THE PRIEST AS PERSON:
A PHILOSOPHY OF
PRIESTLY EXISTENCE

ROBERT E. LAUDER, PH.D.

AFFIRMATION BOOKS
WHITINSVILLE, MASSACHUSETTS

Published With Ecclesiastical Permission

First Edition
©1981 by House of Affirmation, Inc.

Library of Congress Cataloging in Publication Data
Lauder, Robert E.
  The priest as person.
  1. Priests. 2. Catholic Church—Clergy.
I. Title.
BX1912.L338   262 ′.142   81-3665
ISBN 0-89571-013-7   AACR2

Printed by Mercantile Printing Company, Worcester, Massachusetts
United States of America

With prayers for their journeys through life, this book is dedicated to Kwang and Celeste, and to Misop, whose friendship has been a great gift in my life.

CONTENTS

FOREWORD

The Priest As Person is philosophical in approach. Although Affirmation Books usually publishes books concerning the dialogue between psychology and theology, I am encouragd by Father Lauder's approach because I have noted, in my clinical practice, that the lack of insight on the part of many persons in ministry has led to personal frustration and unhappiness. In this book, Father Lauder develops the underlying assumptions of our actions as priests. This development is risky, but if we either refuse or neglect to examine carefully the meaning of our priestly existence, the risk is greater. A healthy, well-developed philosophy of life is the anatomy of human happiness.

The priest in today's world has, as an important part of his ministry, the task of inviting persons to the reflective life. On February 25, 1981, Pope John Paul II gave a homily at the ordination of fifteen priests in Nagasaki, Japan. "It is disconcerting for us, aware as we are of our littleness and sinfulness, to hear addressed to us the clear words: 'You are the light of the world.' The apostles must have trembled at hearing them. So must have other thousands of people since then. And yet, the Lord spoke those words to people whom he knew to be human, limited and sinful. For he also knew that they were to be light, not by their own strength but by reflecting and communicating his light, for he said of himself; 'I am the light of the world.' "

Reading this book will benefit priests, seminarians, and all persons concerned with priestly ministry. The author brings a world of experience to this publication, and Affirmation Books is happy to publish *The Priest As Person*. May this book challenge your thought and encourage your faith.

Thomas A. Kane, Ph.D., D.P.S.
Priest, Diocese of Worcester
Publisher, Affirmation Books
Whitinsville, Massachusetts

March 17, 1981
Feast of St. Patrick

INTRODUCTION

This book attempts to construct a philosophy of the priesthood, an endeavor that may seem strange for many reasons. First, philosophy of any kind, and particularly a philosophy of the priesthood, may seem superfluous in our contemporary world. After all, philosophy, many priests will recall from their days as seminarians, was a dry, abstract discipline that was supposed to be the handmaiden of theology. Philosophy was anything but practical. Indeed its professors and proponents seemed to glory in its impracticality and its extremely speculative caste. As seminarians, we priests had the impression that the more removed a philosophy was from day-to-day living, the better a philosophy it was. It is no wonder then that, as in the early Church Tertullian asked, "What indeed has Athens to do with Jerusalem?," we contemporary priests might ask, "What has philosophy to do with an active ministry?" Our other needs being so many, we may well regard a philosophy of priesthood as irrelevant and unnecessary.

Moreover, never mind the impractical nature of philosophy, a more serious objection to a philosophy of priesthood might focus on the very possibility of such an entity. Because the meaning of Christian priesthood is tied to the meaning of Christ and Christian revelation, a theology of priesthood is possible, but can there be a philosophy of priesthood? Theology is the product of human reflection on Christian revelation. Traditionally, philosophy has been described as an activity of "pure human reason," a reflecting on reality without the direct influence of faith. This understanding of philosophy is certainly the one we priests had when we studied philosophy as seminarians. Because of its proximate relation to God's Word, theology has been called "divine science"; philosophy, because of its distance from faith, has been called merely "human wisdom." Unfortunately, this distinction separates in the minds of some priests the world of faith from the world of philosophy. Because the world of faith is obviously important and is indeed the world in which a Christian lives, works, and prays, the other world can come to be thought of as abstract and unreal. The world of philosophy can be thought of as a "natural world," distinct from the supernatural world of faith; the subject philosophy studies can be thought of as natural man, distinct from the supernatural man on whom faith focuses. Because the real world and real people have been graced and called to a supernatural level, the natural world of philosophy is thought of by many priests as relatively unrelated to human experience.

When my bishop sent me to study philosophy, a number of my priest acquaintances were sorry. They wished that I could study theology rather than philosophy. In their minds, philosophy would be of little service to either me or the Christian community. While regarded as an interesting pastime for those with a speculative caste of mind, philosophy has been judged by many to be of small value to the priest laboring in the vineyard. While some remembered philosophical proofs and arguments might be occasionally drawn on in the construction of an apologetics course or in some discussion with a college student having problems with faith, in general philosophy was judged unhelpful to a priest in the active ministry. Of all the subjects studied in the seminary, philosophy seemed to be the least related to a priest's daily experience.

This book is rooted in the belief that a philosophy of priesthood is neither impractical nor impossible. Let us deal with the second belief first. The neat and clear distinction between philosophy and theology may be more present in textbooks of philosophy than in living thinkers. The history of philosophy is checkered with people whose thought is so religiously oriented that they do not seem to fit neatly under the umbrella of philosophy as traditionally described. While thinkers such as Augustine, Kierkegaard, Buber, and Marcel could be categorized as philosophers according to the traditional description of philosophy, another description of philosophy not only better fits the work of these religious thinkers but allows us to talk about a philosophy of the priesthood. Indeed, it does more than allow us to talk—it encourages us to construct such a philosophy.

In his book entitled *Building the Human*, Robert Johann discusses what the nature of philosophy is for a Catholic believer. Many in the contemporary world think that a Catholic cannot really do philosophy because the believing Catholic already has embraced a whole set of answers to life's most pressing questions. Many Catholics think of philosophy as a pointless pastime because they already know by faith the answers to the questions that philosophy is asking. Rejecting a view of philosophy as a matter of "pure reason" in contrast to theology that proceeds in the light of faith, Johann correctly points out that if this description of philosophy were accurate, then "the Catholic philosopher . . . is one who, in his work at least, suspends his belief or prescinds from it. He tries to operate in the light of reason alone and see how things look from a purely 'natural' point of view."[1] Of course, such a view of philosophy just does not work for the Catholic believer. Johann calls attention to the truth that an individual philosophizes as a person and not as a "pure reason." A Catholic reflects on his or her experience, and that experience has been structured to a great extent by his or her faith. There is no point for a Catholic to try to see things from a natural point of view because a Catholic does not think the natural point of view reveals reality. Can a Catholic, then, really do philosophy? Is not all reflection on experience theology for the Catholic believer? Johann suggests that the serious Catholic believer's reflection must go in two directions. First, he or she must think about what God has revealed and try to grasp its meaning. The subject matter of this reflection is Christian revelation, and the guide is the teaching Church. This type of reflection is theology. However, the individual believer must also reflect on himself or herself as a believer. If the light of faith is looked on not in terms of what it is a response to (God revealing himself) but rather in terms of *who* is making the response, then a new kind of reflection is revealed. A person is responsible for his or her belief and so must try to

---

1. Robert Johann, *Building the Human* (New York: Herder & Herder, 1968), p. 24.

make some sense of why he or she is a believer. Johann writes:

> In other words, I as an individual, relying on my own powers of discernment and unable to place responsibility for my actions on anybody's shoulders but my own, must be able to judge that the very life of faith is a responsible way for a human being to behave. To make this judgment, however, at least to make it explicitly, requires a reflective effort that is directed on the whole structure of human experience, on the exigencies of personal life, and on the demands and impact for the faith, seen not in terms of itself, merely, but as part of experience. And such a reflective effort is, precisely, philosophy.[2]

Because the life of faith is part of experience, it can become along with the rest of experience the proper object of philosophical reflection. In this book, I am philosophizing about personal existence as experienced by priests. Hence the words "priestly existence" in the title. Because priests are responsible for their lives, a philosophy of priestly existence seems an urgent task.

Philosophy is a very personal activity. The image of it as impractical is quite inaccurate. A philosophy of the person raises the most radical questions about human existence, but it can also provide the most marvelous insights into the meaning of persons. These insights are extremely practical: they move a person to live differently. Again Johann's insights can be helpful:

> Of all human enterprises, philosophical inquiry is the most practical. It is the use of intelligence to liberalize action, to open up new possibilities.
> Philosophy is also passionate. It is spurred by

---

2. Ibid., p. 25.

dissatisfaction with what needs correction, zeal in the communal search for greater sense, joy at new harmonies achieved. It is mind in the service of heart, a discipline in the service of human growth.

Philosophical inquiry is, at its best, an adventure in making life whole.[3]

When it is most profound, philosophy deals with mystery. To philosophize about priestly existence is to raise the most radical kinds of questions. Such philosophizing also unveils the most exciting and inspiring kind of truth.

Every person has a philosophy. To a greater or lesser extent, everyone has decided on the type of life he or she lives and on what is or is not important in that life. Even those who have allowed others to decide for them have *decided* to allow others to direct them. I believe that even though today there are marvelous signs of the Spirit operative in the world, Western man's understanding of himself has so moved away from traditional Christian meanings that both contemporary man and the contemporary world can be described as post-Christian. Priests live their priestly existence and reflect on their priestly existence within this post-Christian world. Their self-understanding can gradually lose the Christian dimension that distinguishes it. The post-Christian atmosphere can slowly swallow priests so that they no longer have the insight or support to continue living priestly existence. This small book is offered to priests as an antidote to the post-Christian atmosphere that surrounds them. I am encouraged to put my thoughts on paper, to philosophize in print, only because of the extraordinarily favorable response I have received from fellow priests when the content of this book was presented in lecture form.

---

3. Ibid., p. 11.

I

PERSONS IN A SECULAR WORLD

The view of personhood that I will present in this book strongly emphasizes the relational nature of personal existence. In succeeding chapters, I will try to explore the meaning of the relational dimension of persons and connect that relational dimension to the meaning of truth, freedom, and love. I have chosen each topic because of its implications for priestly existence.

Before examining the mystery of personal existence, it seems wise to sketch the secular atmosphere within which a priest must function and minister. If there is a crisis of the priesthood, then secularism is one of the key causes of that crisis. Numerous illustrations could be offered to reveal that the contemporary atmosphere is secular. The spirit of the age is secular. I am aware that there are signs of a religious revival. Conversations with some of my friends who are parish priests suggest that some wonderful things are happening in parishes. People's lives are being dramatically changed, conversions are taking place, a new interest in prayer is evident among many. These encouraging signs are just a few that could be mentioned. Yet in spite of all the encouraging signs, my honest belief is that the spirit of the age is still secular.

I discuss the spirit of our age not for academic purposes but rather to make crystal clear what is perhaps the chief obstacle to priestly ministry in today's world. Although the expression "spirit of the age" can seem vague and nebulous, the reality is quite concrete and influential. In a book entitled *Naming the Whirlwind: The Renewal of God-Language*, in which he explores and explains contemporary secularism in detail, Langdon Gilkey explains: "When we speak, as we just have, of the 'spirit,' 'mind,' 'mood' or 'Geist' of our culture, we refer to that deep, preconceptual attitude toward and understanding of existence which dominates and forms the cultural life of an epoch, the way men of a given time characteristically apprehend the world they live in and their place within it; their fundamental self-understanding of their being in the world."[1] The spirit of an age is so strong and powerful that it influences everything that takes place within that age—the literature, art, music, philosophy, religion. Of course, it is not necessary that an individual directly study the spirit of his or her age to be influenced by it. Merely to exist within the age is to be influenced by its spirit.

Numerous references could be offered to illustrate the causes that have led to the outlook that pervades our culture. Various key thinkers could be discussed and their in-

---

1. Langdon Gilkey, *Naming the Whirlwind: The Renewal of God-Language* (Indianapolis and New York: Bobbs-Merrill, 1969), p. 3.

fluence could be charted and explained. Gilkey traces these developments, as do William Barrett in *Irrational Man,* David Tracy in *A Blessed Rage for Order,* and Francis Tyrrell in *Man: Believer and Unbeliever.*[2] Most contemporary philosophical movements—pragmatism, linguistic analysis, and existentialism—have contributed to the mood of secularism. During the last one hundred years, most of the more important philosophical thinkers who have had a wide influence have been atheists. The implications of this fact for the religious believer and especially for the "professional religious," such as a priest, are enormous. Rather than analyze individual thinkers, I will sketch in broad strokes the secular atmosphere that surrounds the contemporary Christian.

In *Irrational Man,* Barrett points out that the central fact of the modern history of the West, that is, history from the end of the middle ages to the present time, is the decline of religion.[3] We should not allow this important truth to be clouded over by talk of a religious revival. I am not denying the possibility of a religious revival, but the decline of religion is a deep and more subtle phenomenon than can be erased by quoting statistics about who does or does not believe in God, who does or does not attend church.[4] The decline of religion has penetrated to the psyche of modern man.

---

2. William Barrett, *Irrational Man* (Garden City, N.Y.: Doubleday Anchor Book, 1962); David Tracy, *A Blessed Rage for Order* (New York: Seabury, 1975); Francis Tyrrell, *Man: Believer and Unbeliever* (New York: Alba House, 1974).
3. Barrett, pp. 24ff.
4. Tyrrell, p. 42.

MOVEMENTS CONTRIBUTING
TO DECLINE OF RELIGION

Barrett believes that the three strong movements that have led us from the middle ages into the modern world are Protestantism, science, and capitalism. The key contribution of Protestantism was to tear away the religious symbolism that permeated the cosmos to leave us, albeit with the best of religious intentions, just a cosmos. Protestantism's suspension of reason makes it a strange bedfellow of science. Yet the latter as expressed in the spirit of Enlightenment contributed, along with the religious movement of Protestantism, to leaving man with a world that could be comprehended without any appeal to faith. Barrett correctly comments:

> In secular matters, however—and particularly in its relation toward nature—Protestantism fitted in very well with the new Science. By stripping away the wealth of images and symbols from medieval Christianity, Protestantism unveiled nature as a realm of objects hostile to the spirit and to be conquered by puritan zeal and industry. Thus Protestantism, like science, helped carry forward that immense project of modern man: the despiritualization of nature, the emptying it of all the symbolic images projected upon it by the human psyche.[5]

Capitalism in its own way encouraged people to rationally order and control the world. The process of rationally controlling the world for efficiency and economic profit is, of course, capitalism's goal. Barrett points out that it achieved this goal through the gathering of labor into fac-

---

5. Barrett, p. 27.

tories and the masses of people into cities. This grouping led to the technical control of life and to "the attempt rationally to control public demand by elaborate and fantastic advertising, mass pressure, and even planned sociological research."[6] The modern world that the Enlightenment and the glorification of science, the Protestant denigration of symbols, and capitalism's rational ordering of society have delivered to us is a world in which faith seems to have no role. Obviously, this result was not the intention of the Protestant reformers, but their severing of faith from reason and their denigration of symbols contributed to it. A detailed historical treatment of how we arrived where we are is of less interest for our purposes than a clear picture of our place of arrival. The world we inhabit is a world from which God is absent. Barrett accurately describes this world:

> The decline of religion in modern times means simply that religion is no longer the uncontested center and ruler of man's life, and that the Church is no longer the final and unquestioned home and asylum of his being. The deepest significance of this change does not even appear principally at the purely intellectual level, in loss of belief, though this loss due to the critical inroads of science has been a major historical cause of the decline. The waning of religion is a much more concrete and complex fact than a mere change in conscious outlook; it penetrates the deepest strata of man's total psychic life. . . . Religion to medieval man was not so much a theological system as a solid psychological matrix surrounding the individual's life from birth to death, sanctifying and enclosing all its ordinary and extraordinary occasions

---

6. Ibid., p. 30.

in sacrament and ritual. The loss of the Church was the loss of a whole system of symbols, images, dogmas, and rites which had the psychological validity of immediate experience, and within which hitherto the whole psychic life of Western man had been safely contained. In losing religion, man lost the concrete connection with a transcendent realm of being; he was set free to deal with this world in all its objectivity. But he was bound to feel homeless in such a world, which no longer answered the needs of his spirit.[7]

ABSENCE OF CHRISTIAN CULTURE

One way of underlining the secularism of contemporary consciousness is to remind ourselves that once there was a Christian culture. There was a time when culture corresponded to Christian theology. Both symbolized and presented the same meanings to people. These symbols and meanings permeated people's consciousness, delivered to people a sense of their identity, and underlined the significance of their life and work. Contemporary man is post-Christian: he looks back at Christian culture as radically different from his own. He may feel a nostalgia for such a culture, but he cannot find it among the influences that affect his life. Perhaps nowhere is the absence of Christian culture more evident than in the realm of art.

One will have a difficult search if he or she looks to literature, theatre, or film for works of art with a Christian dimension. Of course, there are exceptions. The novels of Walker Percy or Piers Paul Read, an occasional play such as *A Man For All Seasons* or even *The Elephant Man*, the

---

7. Ibid., pp. 24-25.

films of French director Robert Bresson or John Huston's film version of Flannery O'Connor's *Wise Blood*, and other works that appear sporadically are isolated islands in a sea of secularism.

In a perceptive and provocative article, Richard Blake surveyed the media and concluded that secularism dominated the scene.[8] Blake gathered one of the most telling bits of information from Ben Stein's *The View from Sunset Boulevard*.[9] Stein claims that every one of the television writers and directors he interviewed dismissed all religion as irrelevant. Not one could recognize any influence of religious values in his own life. These are the creative artists whose work filters into living rooms around the country. Indicating that Catholics fare poorly in the books that make the best-seller list, Blake writes:

> Novels about tyrannical, rosary-squeezing nuns, ignorant pastors, alcoholic fathers and battered, submissive mothers are staples of the best-seller lists. Adolescent traumas in the confessional are no longer interesting, but they go on in the mad drive toward self-exorcism. Mary O'Malley's play, a hit in London, is entitled "Once a Catholic," and is based on her experiences in growing up in a boarding school run by Irish nuns. The buffo character is a sex obsessed nun who teaches biology and refuses to answer any questions about reproduction. It lasted for six performances in New York, perhaps because Jimmy

---

8. Richard Blake, "Christians, Lions and the Media," *America* 142 (Jan. 12, 1980): 8-11.

9. Ben Stein, *The View from Sunset Boulevard* (New York: Basic Books, 1979).

Breslin, Peter Hamill, Tom McHale, John Gregory
Dunne and a host of others had already been around
that track so many times before.[10]

After illustrating malicious bigotry in the media and also
the abysmal ignorance of religion that characterizes the
mentality of many who create the media, Blake concludes
that in the media world religion fares very poorly.

These scattered observations do point to at least
one tentative conclusion. The contemporary secularist, and the ex-Catholic aspiring to become a secularist, is reluctant to make any distinction between
good religion and bad religion. It is all the same
thing, otherworldly, irrational and potentially dangerous. The Ayatollah Khomeni, Jonestown, Jimmy
Carter's Sunday School, Mother Teresa and the
Inquisition are all parts of the same pre-Enlighten-
ment fabric. When secular values work in a religious
contest, there is hope for salvation, but religion is
almost always an obstacle to salvation.[11]

The secularized consciousness of contemporary creative
artists is perhaps most obvious when they deal with problems that traditionally would beg for religious solutions.
Today artists do not even raise the topic of religion. In
Michael Cristoffer's Pulitzer-Prize-winning play, *The
Shadow Box*, the subject of death is dramatically explored.
The plot involves three victims of cancer who have entered
a special campus-like residence for terminally ill cancer patients. Their families can stay with them in small cottages
as they prepare for death. Very powerfully, through the
victims' relationships with spouses, parents, and friends,

10. Blake, p. 10.
11. Ibid.

the human mysteries of life, love, and death are explored. Though the theme of death is played and re-played from every angle, the subjects of religion and personal immortality beyond the grave are never brought up by anyone. The playwright's characters never mention the topics. The closest that they come occurs at the end of the play. All the characters turn toward the audience and, in choruslike fashion, intersperse remarks about life and death with the repeated affirmation "yes." Of course, the "yes" indicates a positive approach to life. Yet that positive approach silently excludes religion or any doctrine of resurrection. I had the sense that in the mind of the playwright any reference to resurrection would somehow minimize the meaning of life and death. I wonder how many who see the play either notice or reflect on the fact that the topic of personal immortality is never mentioned.

Two recent films, each nominated for nine Academy Awards in the 1980 balloting, underline the secularized consciousness of serious artists. *Kramer vs. Kramer* explores the breakup of a marriage; *All That Jazz* charts the life of a present-day, extremely successful director of films and plays. As film both works are technically excellent. Their construction, the writing, the acting, the direction— all are exceptionally good. But what is most interesting for our purposes is that in neither film is religion or God mentioned even though both films dramatize the most radical and existential human experiences and problems. What makes the absence of any reference to religion or God so striking is that the mystery of interpersonal relationships, of love, of death are explored so deeply and dramatized so well. I wonder if, in the minds of the creators of the films, religion and God seem so irrelevant that they are not worth a mention.

Hollywood's failure to capture religious mystery is sketched in a provocative article by Andrew Greeley in the *New York Times*.[12] Greeley comments:

> The good religious film has eluded the American industry. To be sure, there has been no shortage of spectaculars ("The Ten Commandments," "King of Kings" and "Joan of Arc" in various manifestations), to say nothing of Biblical sexploitations ("David and Bathsheba," "Samson and Delilah"), tearjerkers ("Miracle of the Bells"), cloying chronicles of clerical culture ("Going My Way," "The Bells of St. Mary's," "Keys of the Kingdom," "Come to the Stable," "The Nun's Story"), ventures into the occult ("Heaven Can Wait," "The Exorcist"), and films with religious background for exotic effect ("Nashville," "A Woman Under the Influence"). American filmmakers have produced movies about religion, movies which exploit religion to titillate or terrify, but no religious movies.[13]

One does not have to agree with Greeley's descriptions of each film to agree with his main point. Certainly, the specific problem that American filmmakers have with the priesthood was clear in Stanley Kramer's *The Runner Stumbles*.[14] Though the camera caught some of the externals of a priest's life and the film raised some questions

---

12. Andrew Greeley, "Why Hollywood Never Asks the God Question," *New York Times*, Jan. 18, 1976, Arts and Leisure.
13. Ibid., p. 1.
14. In *Sign* magazine, "God and Man at the Movies," December 1979-January 1980, pp. 34-38, I analyzed Kramer's film and emphasized that its depiction of religion was at best inadequate.

about the meaning of a priest's life, there was little evidence of any understanding of the mystery and meaning of priestly existence. Probably with no malice on the part of anyone connected with making the film, the mystery of a priest's life was missed. Another striking example of the film industry's inability to deal with religious mystery is illustrated in films made from Graham Greene's novels.[15]

In Peter Shaffer's powerful play *Equus*, the exploration of the young psychotic's passion for horses suggests some commitment to what is more than human, and the psychiatrist's disillusionment with science underlines the philosophical questions that gird the play. Yet the closest that either Shaffer or his psychiatrist can come to the religious issue is to raise questions. At the end of the play, the psychiatrist turns to the audience and says what might serve as a lament of many inhabitants of our post-Christian culture.

> All right—I surrender! I say it! . . . In an ultimate sense I cannot know what I do in this place—yet I do ultimate things. Essentially I cannot know what I do—yet I do essential things. Irreversible, terminal things. I stand in the dark with a pick in my hand, striking at heads! I need—more desperately than my children need me—a way of seeing in the dark. What way is this? . . . *What dark is this?* . . . I cannot call it ordained of God: I can't get that far. I will however pay it so much homage. There is now, in my mouth, this sharp chain. And it never comes out.

The psychiatrist's questions suggest how far the contemporary world has strayed from the Christian vision of life.

---

15. See my article, "The Graham Greene That Eludes the Camera," *New York Times,* March 9, 1980.

Pointing out that in today's society there are committed believers, Tyrrell notes that they are a diminishing breed.

> They are swimming against the tide. The dominant current of our culture, rather than supporting them, as it would have in the past, threatens to submerge them. The day of mass Christianity, of mass Catholicism is over, even on this continent. Social pressure no longer coerces the irresolute to adopt a Christian identity for protective coloration. It is perfectly respectable to be non-religious, and in certain circles, especially among the intellectuals, it is quite disreputable or at least eccentric to be anything else. It would appear that we are fast approaching in this country the situation which already obtains in most of Europe where believers pursue their distinctive commitments on the fringes rather than at the heart of the world in which they live.[16]

THE VISION OF SECULAR HUMANISM

The secular world view is a vision. It includes within it a metaphysics, a philosophy of human nature, and an ethics.[17] The metaphysics is a complete naturalism. There is nothing but nature according to the secularist. To speak of the supernatural is to speak of the meaningless. It is also necessarily to detract from this world and its problems. For the secularist, questions of a Divine Creator are not entertained. In some cases, the very secular atmosphere makes such questions irrelevant. Whatever the current scientific theory of the origin of the universe, it suffices for the secu-

---

16. Tyrrell, pp. 43-44.
17. See John McMahan, "What Does Christianity Add to Secular Humanism," *Cross Currents* 18 (Spring 1968): 129-34, for an excellent explanation of secular humanism.

larist. The world insofar as it can be explained is explained by the active nature of matter. All is material. What in previous religious ages might have been attributed to soul or spirit is explicable by appeal to highly developed dynamic matter. Evolution has gotten us to our present state. The masterpiece of evolution, the human species, is now in charge of the process. Humanity's task is to build a better world.

Even though the secularist is a materialist, he or she is not necessarily a determinist. A good number of secularists recognize personal freedom and attribute it to the highly refined brain and nervous system that evolution has provided human beings. That human persons are free makes them the rulers of the material universe. That they have no goal beyond the grave does not mean that they have no goals. In fact, the very belief that there is no life beyond the grave makes this earthly life especially precious and important. The goals that human beings set for themselves ought to be drawn from human experience. The main goal might be stated as the fullest, richest development of human persons. Everything that fosters human growth can be looked on as a good. So the secularist wants to wipe out poverty, promote mental health, foster good relations among the races, and especially do everything possible to promote education on all levels. For many secularists, education is the new salvation. The only goals that are irrelevant and cannot be promoted are the specifically religious goals.

If secularists had no ethic, they would pose little threat to religious believers. The secularist ethical system is based on experience. There is no appeal to a supernatural revelation or to God. If human experience reveals that something promotes human growth, it is moral; if human experience reveals that something prevents or stifles human growth, then it is immoral. Of course, there are no absolutes. What was immoral one hundred years ago, such as birth control or abortion, may not be immoral today. The standard of judgment is human experience.

The secularist insists that he or she is promoting love among peoples as much as the Christian believer, in fact more so. Because of their belief in a life after death, during which they will be rewarded, Christian believers may not really love people. At least their love is suspect. They may not genuinely love people but may be merely acting out their desires to reach heaven. They may be subtly using people as stepping stones toward their eternal reward.

In a calm setting, perhaps the halls of academe, the Christian believer could argue, I believe quite successfully, with the secular humanist on every point of difference between secularism and Christianity. However, Christians rarely have that opportunity. They must try to preserve and defend their faith among contemporaries whose consciousness has been colored. Simply put, secular humanism is in the air. Even among those who never read its philosophers, perhaps have never even heard of them, the secularistic vision has taken root. It is not necessary that contemporary people be aware of the meaning of the expression "secular humanism"; but they are being bombarded by it nevertheless.

THE SECULAR THREAT

Every Christian is threatened by the vision of secular humanism. A Christian will have a difficult time allowing the hour of worship in church on Sunday to affect his or her consciousness throughout the week. There is very little in contemporary society that supports the message that the Christian hears proclaimed on a Sunday morning. In our society, what supports a couple trying to live a Christian marriage, trying to be a sign, as St. Paul urges, of Christ and the Church to others? There is neither a Christian dogma nor a Christian belief that is not subtly threatened by contemporary secularism.

Though every Christian is threatened by secular humanism, the priest is particularly vulnerable, yet not because he is intellectually less capable of combating it. Because of his training, he is more capable than most people. He is particularly vulnerable because, as the leader and spokesman of the community, as the person who is a professional religious, he will be especially sensitive to an atmosphere in which religion is looked on as irrelevant.

The contemporary priest can be worn down by contemporary secularism. Rather subtly, he can be persuaded to suspect that priestly ministry is worthless, that both his vision and his service are of no real value. He can be persuaded that he is representing an outmoded institution and an archaic morality. He can come to view his celibate existence as a meaningless burden, the sacraments as meaningless symbols.

The contemporary priest has a double problem: to battle the secularism that may be drowning his flock and to battle the secularism that is threatening his very priestly existence. His very awareness of the double threat can be a great step in the right direction. To become aware of the secularistic atmosphere that surrounds his ministry is to take the first step toward transcending secularism. Within the mystery of his priestly existence, the contemporary priest has all the resources he needs not only to survive but to have an extremely rich personal life.

II

EXISTENTIAL VIEW OF PERSONAL EXISTENCE AND PRESENCE

Though it is a generalization, it seems true to say that today most Catholic apologetics centers around the meaning of the human.[1] Catholic theologians believe that it is through reflection on and analysis of the human mystery that they can best open discussion on the meaning of the Catholic faith. Because of this belief, theological anthropology has developed in recent years into one of the most important branches of theology. No less a thinker than Karl Rahner roots his entire theological system in his anthropology.[2]

---

1. For example, Hans Kung, *On Being a Christian,* trans. Edward Quinn (Garden City, N.Y.: Doubleday, 1976); David Tracy, *A Blessed Rage for Order* (New York: Seabury, 1975); and Francis Tyrrell, *Man: Believer and Unbeliever* (New York: Alba House, 1974).
2. Tyrrell, especially pp. 175-87, 196-215.

In this reflection on the meaning and mystery of the priesthood, I will follow the lead of contemporary theologians in their emphasis on the meaning of human existence. I am engaging in a kind of apologetics not for the non-believer but for the priest. I begin with the belief that nothing valuable or insightful that secular humanism says about personal existence need be rejected. I also begin with the belief that my vision of personal existence is more profound, more insightful, and more true than that of the secular humanist. In constructing a philosophy of priestly existence, I will in each chapter first deal with some aspect of personhood and then relate that aspect to priestly existence. The aspect of personal existence that I will explore in this chapter is the very notion of existence and its relation to a world or to a horizon.

RELATIONAL ASPECTS OF HUMAN NATURE

The word "existence" as used in the title of this work and throughout this book has a special meaning. It does not apply to material things or to God.[3] Only human persons exist; things and God do not exist. We are not denying that there are things or that there is a God. We are just denying that they are in the unique way that we are calling existence. We are reserving the word "existence" for the kind of being that is proper to human persons. Though this special use of the word can initially cause some confusion, I

3. William Luijpen, *Existential Phenomenology,* rev. ed., (Pittsburgh: Duquesne University Press, 1969), p. 62. I should like to acknowledge my indebtedness to Father Luijpen. His thinking has profoundly influenced my thinking. Those familiar with his philosophical vision will see his influence on my thought in these pages.

believe that it calls attention to what is unique about personhood and so the special use of the word is more than justified.

A person exists. Indeed, the nature of personhood is existence. What does this mean? The word existence comes from the Latin words *ex* (outside of) and *sto* (stand). To exist means to stand outside yourself. It means that in your very nature you are relational. That a person exists means that he or she does not just happen to relate to others, but rather that the nature or essence of persons is to relate.

The following are several descriptions of personal existence that are attempts at calling attention to the radical meaning of personal existence: (1) to be existence is to be that type of being who in its being stands outside itself; (2) to be existence is to be that type of being who in its being is relational; (3) to be existence is to be that type of being who in its being is present to others; (4) to be existence is to be that type of being who in its being is open to others; (5) to be existence is to be that type of being who in its being is conscious bodiliness in the world; and (6) to be existence is to be that type of being who in its being is incarnate spirit in the world.

Though the last two expressions may seem to be different from the first four, all are calling attention to the same radical mystery of human personhood. The key words in each of the descriptions are "in its being." We are claiming that to be relational is the nature or essence of personal existence. It is how we find ourselves. We have no choice about it. We can choose how we will relate or to what or to whom we will relate, but we have no choice about whether we will relate. To be a person means to be relational. The specific element implied in each of the six descriptions is human consciousness. It is because of human conscious-ness that persons are open, present, and in relation. For a human person to be conscious is to be conscious *of*. We can never be just conscious. The very nature of human consciousness is that it requires an object. This require-ment is the special significance of the six descriptions of ex-istence. They all point to the truth that a human person, because of consciousness, is always open to others. This openness is the very nature of personal existence.

None of the descriptions apply to material things or God in the way that they apply to human persons. Things are not open to other things; things are not present to other things. In my room, the entire meaning of the chair being three feet from the sofa depends on the presence of a per-son: the chair and sofa have no meaning for one another. God in his being is not necessarily open or present to others.[4] God does not need to create others. Creation, rather than a necessary part of God's being, was a free decision on his part. Only human beings in their very nature are present to others.

PRESENCE INFLUENCES
IDENTITY AND MEANING

The implications of the relational aspect of human nature are enormous. Of all the expressions we have been using to capture the meaning of personal existence—''pres-ence,'' ''openness,'' ''in relation to,'' ''standing outside of''—perhaps the most fruitful is presence. Persons cannot decide whether they will be present to others. Wherever

4. Of course, we know from Revelation that the Three Persons are necessarily related to each other.

persons are, they are present to others. They can choose which others and how they will be present. When, where, and how a person is present has a powerful influence on the identity of the person. Two examples may illustrate and clarify this point.

Imagine a young boy growing up in the slums of an inner city. His parents are separated. The mother with whom the boy lives is a kind person but of limited intelligence and emotional strength. The boy's playmates come from similar backgrounds. The schools he attends are educationally inferior, the teachers not exceptionally dedicated. This description is a partial picture of the boy's world. Obviously, that world, to which he is present, will have a strong influence on his development. While not opting for some form of determinism, we must admit that this boy will be influenced by the world to which he is present. A few lines from W. H. Auden's poem, "The Shield of Achilles," suggest something of the possible bleakness of such a child's world.

> That girls are raped, that two boys knife a third,
> Were axioms to him, who'd never heard
> Of any world where promises were kept,
> Or one could weep because another wept.[5]

Next imagine a young girl living in an upper middle-class neighborhood. Both of her parents hold graduate degrees, are deeply in love, and are mature, dedicated parents. She is sent to the best schools. The girl's companions come from backgrounds similar to hers. Once again, though not surrendering to a deterministic view of reality, we must ad-

---

5. W. H. Auden, "The Shield of Achilles," *The New Oxford Book of English Verse* (New York: Oxford University Press, 1972), p. 922.

mit that the world to which the girl is present and open will greatly influence her life. Certainly, the young girl's world is radically different from the world to which the young boy of our first example is open.

The point is that each person lives in his or her own world and has his or her own horizon. By world or horizon, I mean a network of meanings that are real and important to an individual. In the six descriptions of personal existence, the basic other that a person is "open to," "present to," or "in relation to" is meaning. To be a person is to be an unveiler of meaning, a light on meaning. To be a person is to be open to meaning. The importance of this fact cannot be overemphasized.

A person can be open to the meaning of things, other persons, and God. A person can draw meaning from schools attended, books read, films seen, theatre productions viewed. Often many of the important meanings in a person's life come from parents and teachers. For some people, the meanings proposed by religions are very important and influential. The meanings that come across from a particular culture, *Geist,* or world view can be very powerful in affecting an individual's outlook on life. The network of meanings that are dominant in a person's life or outlook make up that individual's world or horizon. Every person, the most intelligent and the most ignorant, the most dynamic and the dullest, has a world or a horizon. A person's world or horizon may be very broad and exciting or narrow and dull. Bernard Lonergan writes:

> There is a sense in which it may be said that each of us lives in a world of his own. That world usually is a bounded world, and its boundary is fixed by the range of our interests and our knowledge. There are

things that exist, that are known to other men, but about them I know nothing at all. There are objects of interest that concern other men, but about them I could not care less. So the extent of our knowledge and the reach of our interests fix a horizon. Within that horizon we are confined.

Such confinement may result from the historical tradition within which we are born, from the limitations of the social milieu in which we were brought up, from our individual psychological aptitudes, efforts, misadventures.[6]

The point is that every person is in relation to a world or horizon and even the slowest and dullest person is in relation to a set of meanings that can dynamically develop and change. Of course, the confinement of our horizons that Lonergan mentions is a relative confinement. The entrance of new meanings into our lives can extend and expand our horizons. We can be called into new worlds, and we can freely choose to enter those worlds. The dynamic nature of a person's horizon or world is well revealed by Michael Novak in his book entitled *The Experience of Nothingness:*

A horizon has two poles: the subject and the range of his activities. The point of the horizon metaphor is to link the subject and his world in a mutually defining relationship. It is to refuse to think dualistically of an isolated self over against an external world, a conscious ego trapped inside a bag of skin in a world of colliding objects. What we know of the world is known only through consciousness, and we are conscious only through being in a world. Self and world interpenetrate; neither exists in regard to the other until they are mutually united in act. One pole of my

6. Bernard Lonergan, *The Subject* (Milwaukee: Marquette University Press, 1968), p. 1.

horizon is the range of all I can experience, understand, evaluate and do. The other pole is the subject
of these activities of experiencing, understanding,
evaluating and doing. Neither pole can be attended to
without reference to the other.[7]

The person and his or her world are in a mutually defining relationship. The person brings about his or her world
through presence and openness, and the world greatly influences who the person is and becomes. As a person
changes, his or her world changes; as a world deepens or
becomes shallow, as a horizon expands or narrows, a person changes.

To what or to whom a person is present will greatly affect that person's world or horizon. Our parents, spouses,
children, and friends make tremendous contributions to
the structure of our world. The books we read or do not
read can be influential in structuring our horizons. If a
young man of twenty-five has practiced basketball thirty
or forty hours a week from his early teenage years, then he
will be very at home in the world of basketball. In that
world, he may be able to do things that seem superhuman
to the rest of us. However, his horizon may be impover-
ished outside the world of basketball. He may not be at
home with ideas and may have a very narrow and limited
vision of life. What he has been present to has greatly affected his world. Another world will be inhabited by an ex-
cessively studious man of twenty-five. If he spends fifty or
sixty hours a week reading and studying, he will probably
be magnificent in the world of scholarship. However, he

---

7. Michael Novak, *The Experience of Nothingness* (New York:
Harper & Row, 1970) p. 27.

may be very ill at ease at parties and other social gatherings. The point is that we pay for our presence: to whom or to what we are present greatly affects our world.

For the structuring of a horizon or world, perhaps even more important than to whom or to what a person is present is how that individual is present. A person is never merely physically present. A person is never merely present the way a thing is present, for example, the way a desk or chair is present. A person is always open to other, present to other. How one is present can take enormously varied forms. One can be present in a loving way or a hostile way, in an interested or bored manner, attentively or distractedly, with faith or disbelief. There seems to be no limit to the number of ways a person can be present.[8] The different ways a person can be present have different effects on a person's world or horizon. Psychologist Rollo May writes:

> *World is the structure of meaningful relationships in which a person exists and in the design of which he participates.* Thus world includes the past events which condition my existence and all the vast variety of deterministic influences which operate upon me. But it is these *as I relate to them,* am aware of them, carry them with me, molding, inevitably forming, building them in every minute of relating. For to be aware of one's world means at the same time to be designing it. . . .

---

8. In his book *Man's Search for Meaning* (New York: Simon and Schuster, 1959), Victor Frankl comments on his experience in a Nazi concentration camp and argues that the manner in which prisoners were present to their suffering led to either their destruction or survival.

World is never something static, something merely
given which the person then "accepts" or "adjusts
to" or "fights." It is rather a dynamic pattern which,
so long as I possess self-consciousness, I am in the
process of forming and designing.[9]

INTENTIONALITY IS CENTRAL

Central to a person's structuring and designing of his or
her world and horizon is the notion of intentionality used
by existential philosophers and psychologists. The word
"intentionality" means more than what a person intends
or wishes. It refers to a stance or perspective or angle of vision that a person takes on reality. There are a seemingly
infinite number of ways of looking at reality, and each way
opens the individual to some set of meanings but simultaneously prevents that individual from seeing other sets of
meanings. In *Love and Existence*, William A. Sadler provides a good example to illustrate the influence of intentionality on a person's world or horizons. In trying to show
that there are no simple facts, no merely objective facts
that are not tied to a particular outlook, stance, or perspective, Sadler quotes a verse from one of Wallace Stevens's
poems:

Twenty men crossing a bridge
Into a village,
Are twenty men crossing twenty bridges,
Into twenty villages.[10]

---

9. Rollo May, "Contributions to Existential Psychotherapy,"
in *Existence*, ed. Rollo May (New York: Simon and Schuster,
1958), pp. 59-60.
10. Quoted in William A. Sadler, *Existence and Love* (New
York: Scribner's, 1969), pp. 10-11.

What does the verse mean? Is it suggesting a subjectivism, a denial that there are objective facts? Sadler makes the same point that I am making in stressing the interaction between a person and his or her world: there are no objective facts apart from subjective stances and perspectives. In other words, all meanings and all worlds are tied to personal presence and the particular intentionality or perspective that a person assumes. Sadler comments on the perspectives or intentionalities that some of the twenty soldiers might have toward the bridge. For one soldier the bridge may be where he kissed his first love, to another it is the bridge off which his father leapt and drowned, to another the bridge leads to the town where his worst enemy lives, to another the bridge is architecturally interesting. There are as many meanings to the bridge as there are human perspectives. Sadler writes:

> To expect that there is only one right answer to the question: What do you see? is to ignore the full situation in general and the facts of meaning in particular. To insist on one set of material facts is to ignore the people and their meaning-laden experience which constitutes that situation. . . . To get at the facts of the situation demands of us that we take into account the human element which makes the situation what it is.[11]

Sadler's example of the twenty men crossing the bridge is one example to illustrate my point about world or horizon: all meanings are personal, that is, all meanings are tied to the intentionality or perspective of a person. Though there are numerous influences on a person affect-

---

11. Ibid., p. 11.

ing his or her horizon or world, the person is finally responsible for that world or horizon. Persons are free, and though they can be strongly influenced, they are not determined.[12] The depth and expansion of our worlds depends to a large extent on our creativity and vitality. We are responsible for our horizons.

> All our knowledge arises from within us, from within our ceaseless encounter with our world. Our knowledge takes its place within a horizon of meaning. This horizon is not determined by external forces. It is infinitely flexible, and its boundaries are set by the creative spirit of men within a limiting situation but not within a fixed, predetermined world.[13]

A PRIEST'S HORIZON OR WORLD

What about the horizon or world of a priest? What are the meanings that contribute to a priest's world? The influence of secularism on a priest's world or horizon is enormous. Within a post-Christian atmosphere, the priest must opt for and sustain meanings that most of his contemporaries no longer embrace. A priest's world or horizon, then, is different from that of his contemporaries. Yet this difference can be said of any Christian. Every person trying to have a Christian horizon in our post-Christian world can experience a crisis of meaning. Because the priest is a leader in the community, because the priest is a professional religious, because the priest's whole life is centered on Christian meaning, his crisis can be especially intense. In fact, it would be strange if some kind of tension

---

12. I will discuss freedom in more detail in Chapter 4.
13. Sadler, pp. 15-16.

were not experienced by a priest in a post-Christian world. One might wonder if the absence of tension suggests that the priest's Christian horizon has been wiped away by the secularism that surrounds him. In trying to stay in dialogue with Christian meaning, a priest has various sources that can help him. Some of these are Christian revelation, scripture, the teaching Church, the sacraments, prayer, spiritual reading, his fellow priests, and the Christian community. A priest tries to sustain a Christian horizon not only for himself. His vocation is to try to help others sustain a Christian horizon. Thus he models his life after that of Jesus.

THREE GOSPEL SCENES

In almost every Gospel scene, Jesus tries to offer new meaning to people. He calls people to enter a new world, to expand their horizons, to accept a new set of meanings. Though just about any Gospel scene would illustrate Jesus' attempt to help people expand their horizons, three examples will suffice: the Samaritan woman at the well (John 4:4-26), Jesus proclaiming the eight beatitudes (Luke 6:20-23), and Jesus teaching his disciples the Our Father (Luke 11:2-4 and Matt. 6:7-13).

At least five times Jesus tries to extend the Samaritan woman's horizon, to call her beyond herself into a new world. He first asks her for a drink of water. She is shocked that he would ask a Samaritan woman for a drink because Jews did not associate with Samaritans. She should be shocked, and perhaps this reaction is part of Jesus' plan to call her beyond herself, to open new meanings to her.

Jesus tries again to call her into a new world when he responds to her comment indicating her surprise that he should ask her for water. Jesus says: "If you only knew what God is offering and who it is that is saying to you: 'Give me a drink,' you would have been the one to ask, and he would have given you living water." Understandably confused, the woman points out to Jesus that he has no bucket and asks if he is greater than Jacob who built the well. Jesus continues to try to deepen her understanding of who he is: "Whoever drinks this water will get thirsty again, but anyone who drinks the water that I shall give will never be thirsty again: the water that I shall give will turn into a spring inside him, welling up to eternal life." Responding to what Jesus says, the woman wants some of the special water about which Jesus has spoken. Her world is beginning to open; her horizon is beginning to expand.

Jesus tries to call her beyond herself a third time when he reveals that he knows that the woman has had five husbands and is living with a sixth man. Jesus is preparing her to be led into a deeper faith-world.

Jesus' response to the woman's remark about the dispute between Jews and Samaritans concerning where to worship is the fourth point at which Jesus opens up new meanings for her. He says: "Believe me, woman, the hour is coming when you will worship the Father neither on this mountain nor in Jerusalem. You worship what you do not know; we worship what we do know; for salvation comes from the Jews. But the hour will come—in fact it is here already—when true worshippers will worship the Father in spirit and truth: that is the kind of worshipper the Father wants. God is spirit, and those who worship must worship in spirit and truth." Jesus has tried to unveil for the woman the essence of worship, the real meaning of worship. He has tried to help her to see that the place of worship is not nearly so important as the attitude of worship.

In response to the woman's remark that she believes that when the Messiah comes he will reveal all truth, Jesus tells her, "I am he." This fifth and final time Jesus tries to open a new world for the Samaritan woman.

This kind of simple analysis of Jesus trying to share his network of meanings with others can be applied throughout the Gospel. Jesus is constantly calling people to transcend themselves and enter into a new world.

With his proclamation of the eight beatitudes, Jesus turns people's values upside down. On several important points, he gives his listeners a new vision of how people should act and what is important in human life, e.g., that they should love their enemies and do good to those who hate them. In the sixth chapter of Luke, Jesus' recitation of the beatitudes follows two scenes revealing the Pharisees' excessive legalism. After recounting these two scenes, Luke mentions that Jesus spent a night in the hills in prayer, then the next day picked his twelve apostles. He came down to a piece of level ground and among a large crowd performed some healings. He then recited the beatitudes. The way Luke situates this scene, the reader realizes that Jesus is telling us a new way to live, is telling us about new meanings that we never knew or at least have forgotten. Clearly, Jesus is trying to expand the horizons of his listeners while Luke is trying to expand the horizons of his readers.

The account of the Our Father in the eleventh chapter of Luke dramatically underlines the fact that Jesus is trying to lead his disciples into a deeper world of meanings. Jesus teaches them the Our Father because one of his disciples requested of him, "Lord, teach us to pray, just as John taught his disciples." In the sixth chapter of Matthew, the Our Father becomes part of a series of teachings that Jesus gives. An analysis of the Our Father suggests the deepest meanings about God and about us. The prayer can open us to God's identity and to our identity.

In scene after scene in the Gospel, Jesus tries to call people beyond themselves into a new world of meanings. This is the role of the priest, who must first, as best he can, enter into Jesus' world, assume Jesus' horizons—"In your minds you must be the same as Christ Jesus" (Phil. 2:5)—and, then, in as many ways as he can, call others into that world. The double task, assuming Jesus' horizon and calling others to assume that horizon, is especially difficult today because of the secularistic meanings that surround both the priest and his flock. The difficulties that surround the contemporary priest can seem insurmountable. Certainly, the most important meanings in his world are not supported by his contemporaries. However, within priestly existence there are resources available not only to survive but to succeed. Christian truth is one of these resources.

III

PRIESTLY EXISTENCE AND TRUTH

Truth has fallen on bad times. A quick way to have any audience expect the abstract, the irrelevant, or the dogmatic is to announce that you wish to discuss the nature or meaning of truth. I know of no important topic that is so misunderstood or poorly appreciated. Contemporary Americans seem either to have surrendered any hope of knowing the truth or to be just not that interested in pursuing truth. For several years, I taught a religion course entitled "Religion and Person" at a secular college. I did not identify myself as a priest because I was afraid that the students might be intimidated and not speak freely. I introduced myself as Dr. Lauder. At the beginning of each semester, I had to work overtime to convince the students that religion had something to do with truth and that the pursuit of truth was not necessarily a hopeless search. The predominant attitude among the students at the start of the course was that only science dealt with truth, that religion dealt largely with feelings. The students had such a subjectivistic attitude toward truth that they saw little purpose in discussing the most radical questions about the meaning of personal existence. Without even investigating, they had decided that truth was beyond reach.[1]

Certainly, priests do not think that truth is beyond reach; nor do they embrace any subjectivistic views of truth. Yet they may half-consciously think of truth as abstract, speculative, and considerably removed from their pastoral lives. Depending on their education in dogmatic theology when they were seminary students, they may even think of dogmatic truth as abstract or irrelevant. I have a vivid recollection of an attitude prevalent among some of my contemporaries when we were seminarians that moral theology was the really important subject because it was more practical than dogma: moral theology helped you to hear confessions while dogmatic theology merely dealt with the truth of revelation. In this discussion of truth, I hope to show that truth is not only relevant to the daily life of a priest but that nothing is more practical than truth. When the relational aspect of personal existence is emphasized, the questions about truth become especially pressing. If a person develops through dialogue with his or her

---

1. It was my happy experience that after the students had been led to reflect on the meaning of truth, and especially on the meaning of religious truth, their attitudes changed radically. In anonymous evaluations of the course, numerous students commented that the course had moved them to change their outlook on religion. The material in the course was similar to the material in this book. In the course, the application of existentialist philosophy was made to personal existence in general rather than explicitly to priestly existence.

world, through dialogue with his or her network of meanings, through dialogue with his or her horizon, then whether these meanings are true or false becomes crucial for the growth of the person.

Without turning this chapter into a lengthy treatment of epistemology, I will sketch five aspects of truth and then apply them to Christian truth and a priest's life and apostolate. The five aspects of truth that seem especially important in this exploration of priestly existence are (1) truth is relational, (2) truth involves responsibility, (3) truth requires commitment, (4) the meaning of essential truth, and (5) truth is fruitful.

TRUTH IS RELATIONAL

The view of truth that I am defending sees truth not as a thing or substance but as the product of an encounter.[2] Truth comes about through a person's encountering what is other than himself or herself. Through the encounter the person sheds light on or unveils the other, and meaning appears. If the person has correctly shed light on the other and correctly articulated that meaning in a judgment, then truth has appeared. The truth has come about through the presence of the person to reality or to some aspect of reality. The route to truth underlines for us the importance of the contribution of the person. Truth is brought about by persons. Therefore truth is radically historical. It begins with the history of persons. Just as we cannot talk about meaning apart from human persons, so we cannot talk about true meaning apart from persons.

---

2. An excellent treatment of truth is present in William Luijpen, *Existential Phenomenology* (Pittsburgh: Duquesne University Press, 1969), pp. 133-77.

TRUTH INVOLVES RESPONSIBILITY

Because truth is unveiled or brought about by the presence of a person, we can say that persons are responsible for the truth in their lives. We are not saying that persons arbitrarily create truth. They must be faithful to the other upon which or whom they are shedding light. They must allow what is there to appear. They must not deny it or distort it or neglect it. What being responsible for the truth in our lives means is that we must be loyal and faithful responders to the truth.

Admitting that there are many factors in a person's life that influence and affect the truth or lack of truth, we are stressing the contribution that the individual makes in bringing about truth. Though influences that contribute to or detract from the truth in a person's world seem unlimited—parents, teachers, schools, books, newspapers, television, friends, enemies—a person either does or does not allow truth to enter his or her world. Persons are either open to the truth or they are not.

TRUTH REQUIRES COMMITMENT

Very much related to a person's responsibility in relation to truth is the notion of commitment. Every truth from the least significant to the most important requires a commitment on the part of the knower. If the individual refuses to make the commitment required, then that person will have to live without that truth. No commitment, no truth. No gift of self, no placing of personal presence in a given situation, no true meaning appears. Discussing meaning, Rollo May writes:

The conclusion, therefore, to which our argument points is that every *meaning has within it a commitment. . . .* Meaning has no meaning apart from intention. Each act of consciousness *tends toward* something, is a turning of the person toward something, and has within it, no matter how latent, some push toward a direction for action.

Cognition, or knowing, and conation, or willing, then go together. We could not have one without the other. This is why commitment is so important. If I do not *will* something, I could never know it; and if I do not *know* something, I would never have any content for my willing. In this sense, it can be said directly that man makes his own meaning. Note that I do not say that he *only* makes his meaning, or that it is not dialectically related at every instant to reality; I say that if he is not engaged in making his meaning, he will never know reality.[3]

An example from the academic world may clarify the point that I am making about commitment. If I wish to master calculus, if I wish to make the truths of calculus part of my life, then I will have to make a commitment. In my case, I will have to take other courses in mathematics in order to prepare myself for a course in calculus. My knowledge of mathematics is so poor, my background in mathematics so weak, that I probably will have to study a long time so that I can master the courses that are preliminary to the study of calculus. Perhaps I do not wish to make that kind of commitment. I might decide that I will not put in the long hours sitting at a desk trying to master the mathematical material. That decision is possible. But if

---

3. Rollo May, *Love and Will* (New York: W. W. Norton, 1969), p. 230.

I make that decision, if I decide not to make that commitment, then I must live without the truths of calculus. Every truth involves a commitment; every truth costs us something.

Perhaps the calculus example seems trivial. But the example of Gospel truth or Christian truth is far from trivial. Gospel truth requires a commitment, a commitment much more difficult than that demanded by calculus. In order to have access to Gospel truth, a person must make a faith commitment. In order to receive Gospel truth, a person must make himself or herself present in faith to Gospel meaning. I mentioned in my discussion of world and horizon that a person can be present in numerous ways. One of the most radical and demanding ways is faith presence whereby a person makes himself or herself present to the Gospel in such a way that he or she is in effect saying, "This is the most important meaning in the world." To believe in the Gospel is to risk everything we have and are on its truth. If we choose not to believe, then we must live without Gospel truth.

Because truth is the product of an event, it happens at a particular moment in time. Students come in contact with great literature when they first open a great book; persons first discover their own impatience when they see the patience of their friends; individuals begin to see the truth of Christianity when they first hear about Jesus. In every instance that truth is uncovered, it happens at a certain moment. Usually that moment must be prepared for, both in the life of the culture and in the life of an individual. One must prepare oneself for the truths of the Gospel. Lack of such preparation may mean that truth is not unveiled, that moments of truth are missed.

By stressing a person's responsibility for truth and the need for a commitment, we are implying that a price must be paid for truth. Every truth—the least significant and the most important—will cost the knower something. If the person is not ready tó pay the price, then the truth will not be available. If a person does not make himself or herself present in the way required for a particular truth, then the moment of truth will pass by him or her. I believe that the more important and meaningful the truth, the more demanding and difficult the presence that is required. So with the slightest and least difficult and demanding presence I can determine whether it is raining. A more difficult presence is required if I wish to know the meaning of some poem or some play by Shakespeare. When I decided to read James Joyce's *Ulysses*, I discovered that I had to make myself present to an entire course on Joyce if I wanted to unveil the meanings in Joyce's great book. I could not grasp the truth in Joyce's *Ulysses* as easily as I can grasp the truth about whether it is raining. Gospel truth demands an even more profound self-gift, an even more generous presence.

THE MEANING OF ESSENTIAL TRUTH

A distinction can be made between two types of truth. I will call one factual truth and the other essential truth. As its name suggests, factual truth means the facts of some situation. Factual truth may be very difficult to come by, for example, finding out who committed a crime or discovering the correct date of a document. But once a factual truth is discovered, it is not difficult to understand. Essential truth, which refers to the radical and basic meaning of some reality, can be both difficult to come by and difficult to understand after it is discovered.

It is usually difficult to discover what people we know are really like; it is usually difficult to come to know ourselves; it is difficult to come to know God. Even if we discover essential truths about others, ourselves, or God,[4] we will never understand any of those truths perfectly. There is a depth to essential truth that cannot be exhausted. Christian revelation and Gospel truth deal with essential truth. They deal with the meaning of God and the meaning of us. Through the Christ event—Jesus' life, death, and resurrection—truths about God and us have been revealed. These truths are so deep that we will never exhaust their meaning. Of course, we can become so preoccupied with factual truth that some of the most important essential truths, such as truths about other people or about interpersonal relationships, become absent from our lives. There is a danger that our knowledge becomes so superficial that we are really not concerned with any truths.

Writing about the dangers of living in a technological society, William Barrett makes some telling points about truth. He says that technology can cause us to be preoccupied with things and with false needs. He writes:

> All of this makes for an extraordinary externalization of life in our time. The tempo of living is heightened, but a greed for novelties sets in. The machinery of communication makes possible the almost instantaneous conveying of news from one point on the globe to another. People read three or four editions of a daily paper, hear the news on the radio, or see tomorrow morning's news on their television screen

---

4. We are not claiming that we know God's essence. The term essential truth is used in relation to God to indicate we know some true meanings about him.

at night. Journalism has become a great god of the period, and gods have a way of ruthlessly and demonically taking over their servitors. In thus becoming a state of mind—as Kierkegaard prophesied it would do, writing with amazing clairvoyance more than a century ago—journalism enables people to deal with life more and more at second hand. Information usually consists in half-truths, and "knowledgeability" becomes a substitute for real knowledge. Moreover, popular journalism has by now extended its operations into what were previously considered the strongholds of culture—religion, art, philosophy. Every man walks around with a pocket digest of culture in his head. The more competent and streamlined journalism becomes, the greater its threat to the public mind—particularly in a country like the United States. It becomes more and more difficult to distinguish the secondhand from the real thing, until most people end by forgetting there is such a distinction. The very success of technique engenders a whole style of life for the period, which subsists purely on externals. What lies behind those externals —the human person, in its uniqueness and its totality—dwindles to a shadow and a ghost.[5]

In order to develop as a person, an individual must be open to essential truth.

TRUTH IS FRUITFUL

There is nothing so practical as truth. Error frustrates us, hinders our development, slows down our growth; truth helps us to move fruitfully into the future. All truths do this. From the simplest truths of everyday living, such

---

5. William Barrett, *Irrational Man* (Garden City, N.Y.: Double-day Anchor Book, 1962), p. 32.

as how to run machines in a home so that daily household chores get done, to the most important religious truths— all are fruitful in moving us into the future. If I want to clean the house but do not know how to run the vacuum cleaner, I experience frustration. What should be an aid to cleaning the house quickly becomes an obstacle. I spend the whole day trying to figure out how to work the machine. If I knew the truth about how to run it, I could use my time more fruitfully.

Religious truth also works. It can humanize us, personalize us, and open us up to God. Rather than being speculative, religious truth is the most practical type of truth because it has the greatest capacity to change us. Christian revelation and Gospel truth tell us the most important meanings about ourselves, others, and God. Christian truth tells us who God is and who we are. Christian truth reveals in Jesus both the meaning of humanity and the meaning of divinity. By looking at Jesus, the Christian can learn who the Father is. Jesus said to Philip: ''To have seen me is to have seen the Father'' (John 14:9). Taking Jesus' comment to Philip as a comment to each of us, we can remind ourselves that everything Jesus did, he did as Son and as the Word of the Father. Jesus is the model of human living whom the Father has sent us.

Bernard Cooke has written the following about Jesus as Word:

> It means that this man, Jesus of Nazareth, is the Father's own proper Word spoken humanly so that men might receive the gift of the Father himself. The function of ''word'' in any context is to establish communication through mutual understanding: this is preeminently verified in the case of God's own word—he is the light that is the life of men (John 1:4),

sent because the Father so loved men (John 3:16), sent to bear witness to the truth that will liberate men (John 8:32).

In telling us that God the Father's own divine Son is his Word, Christian revelation is pointing to the mysterious fact that the Father images forth his own identity in this Son who is his total self-expression (Col. 1:15). It is this Word, who expresses his fatherhood even in the inner life of the Godhead, whom the Father speaks to men in Jesus. This man Jesus, who himself is uniquely for all other men at the same time that he is totally oriented to his Father, reveals in himself the correlative facts that God is for men and that man in the deepest reaches of his existence is a being for God.[6]

JESUS IS THE TRUTH THAT CHALLENGES

Everything Jesus does, he does as Son and Word and that means everything Jesus does reveals the truth about God to us. If we wish to know the truth about God, we can look to his Word. However, Jesus does not merely reveal the truth about God to us. He also reveals to us the truth about self and neighbor. To forget this fact might be to change Jesus into a kind of idol, an idol that cannot challenge us because it does not speak to us about ourselves. Theologian John Shea, in discussing Jesus as the truth that challenges us, as "the deepest truth about us," stresses that Jesus is the revelation of humanity as well as of God. Pointing out that in our very naming of Jesus there lurks the danger that we will cloud the challenge, Shea suggests that the process by which this happens to Jesus might be called "hardening."

---

6. Bernard Cooke, *Beyond the Trinity* (Milwaukee: Marquette University Press, 1969), pp. 39-40.

The metaphor to use for this process which has happened to Jesus is hardening. The fluid Jesus who flowed into both God and humankind has gradually hardened into a self-contained mold. In a very real sense rigor mortis has set in. The ultimate perversion of Jesus is that he can now be considered without God being revealed or humankind being grasped. In this context Jesus becomes a divine fact to be taken into account rather than a revelation to be encountered. As a fact, even a wonderful fact, he remains information and can be approached with the one attitude his contemporaries would not even manage toward Him—indifference. What has plagued recent Catholicism is a conceptually concise Son of God who does not entice us into the world of his Father.[7]

We might try to reduce Jesus to factual truth rather than essential truth because then we will more easily control him. If we allow the essential truth that Jesus is revealing to enter our lives, then we are going to have to change. The essential truth of Jesus will challenge us in a way that no factual truth can challenge us.

John's Gospel and epistles are especially illuminative concerning Christian truth. John stresses that we should watch Jesus and so gradually come to grasp and see into the truth that Jesus reveals. In John's vision of truth, Jesus receives the truth from his Father. In his behavior as man, Jesus is profoundly influenced by the Father's unique presence to him. "As it is, you want to kill me when I tell you the truth as I have learned it from God" (John 8:40). Jesus refers to his special relationship with the Father and the importance of accepting what he teaches:

7. John Shea, *The Challenge of Jesus* (New York: Doubleday Image Book, 1977), pp. 39-40.

He who comes from heaven bears witness to the things he has seen and heard, even if his testimony is not accepted; though all who do accept his testimony are attesting the truthfulness of God, since he whom God has sent speaks God's own words: God gives him the Spirit without reserve. (John 3:31-34)

If anyone hears my words and does not keep them faithfully, it is not I who shall condemn him, since I have come not to condemn the world, but to save the world; he who rejects me and refuses my words has his judge already: the word itself that I have spoken will be his judge on the last day. For what I have spoken does not come from myself; no, what I was to say, what I had to speak, was commanded by the Father, who sent me, and I know that his commands mean eternal life. And therefore what the Father has told me is what I speak. (John 12:47-50)

A detailed exegesis of any of these texts is not necessary to see that Jesus encounters God in a special way, has a special relationship with the Father, and, because of that encounter and relationship, is the recipient of God's truth. Having received God's truth, Jesus feels compelled to pass that truth on to others. In contrast to Jesus, the prince of evil is referred to in John as the inventor of lies and the father of lies:

Do you know why you cannot take in what I say? It is because you are unable to understand my language. The devil is your father, and you prefer to do what your father wants. He was a murderer from the start; he was never grounded in the truth; there is no truth in him at all: when he lies he is drawing on his own store, because he is a liar, and the father of lies. But as for me, I speak the truth and for that very reason, you do not believe me. Can one of you convict me of sin? If I speak the truth, why do you not believe me? (John 8:43-46)

There is then a kind of battle between Jesus and the father of lies, a battle between the truth that Jesus presents and the untruth presented by the father of lies. For those who accept his truth, Jesus makes some extraordinary promises: "I tell you most solemnly, whoever keeps my word will never see death" (John 8:51).

Of course, John goes much further than merely saying that Jesus has a special truth to hand on. He attributes these words to Jesus: "I am the Way and the Truth and the Life" (John 14:6). What does it mean that Jesus is the Truth?

Though our age or culture can play down the importance of ultimate questions, it seems that those questions will eventually rear their annoying heads. The secularistic atmosphere that surrounds us plays down the importance of ultimate questions, but it cannot seem to totally silence the yearning of the human heart. When that yearning is recognized, ultimate questions appear. John Shea, commenting on John's statement that Jesus is the Truth, writes:

> Jesus is not only a pathway into the mystery of existence but he is the truth about that existence. The type of truth which Jesus is goes beyond accurate information, a flawless accounting of facts. Jesus is the truth in the sense that he uncovers what is hidden, brings to light the last dimension of human existence which so often remain in darkness.[8]

The truth that Jesus reveals, the truth that Jesus is, is the most fruitful truth because it is the most radical, the most existential, the most ultimate. Not only in what he says is

---

8. Shea, p. 43.

Jesus the truth, but in what he does and is Jesus reveals the meaning of God to us and the meaning of ourselves to us.

Of course, the meaning of Jesus, of God, and of ourselves becomes most evident in the Easter events. In order that people might grasp and enter into the meaning of the Easter mystery, John stresses that the Spirit has been given to us. This Spirit is the Spirit of Truth. John stresses the role of the Spirit in Jesus' mission, the role of the Spirit in making known the truth that Jesus was sent to bring, the truth that Jesus is. Jesus said to his followers:

> If anyone loves me he will keep my word, and my Father will love him, and we shall come to him and make our home with him. Those who do not love me do not keep my word. And my word is not my own; it is the word of the one who sent me. I have said these things while still with you; but the Advocate, the Holy Spirit, whom the Father will send in my name, will teach you everything and will remind you of all I have said to you. (John 14:23-26)

> I still have many things to say to you but they would be too much for you now. But when the Spirit of truth comes he will lead you to the complete truth, since he will not be speaking as from himself but will say only what he has learnt; and he will tell you of the things to come. (John 16:12-13)

The role of Jesus' apostles is to bear witness to Jesus and his Spirit.

> I call you friends, because I have made known to you everything I have learnt from my Father. You did not choose me, no, I chose you; and I commissioned you to go out and bear fruit, fruit that will last; and then the Father will give you anything you ask him in my name. (John 15:15-17)

> Consecrate them in the truth, your word is truth. As
> you sent me into the world, I have sent them into the
> world, and for their sake I consecrate myself in that
> they too may be consecrated in truth. I pray not only
> for these, but for those also who through their words
> will believe in me. (John 17:17-20)

The followers of Jesus are to be consecrated in truth.
The truth that Jesus has brought, the truth that Jesus is,
should become the center of their lives. The followers of
Jesus must open themselves to the Holy Spirit, who will
teach them the truth Jesus has revealed. The Father has revealed the truth to Jesus and through Jesus to others. By
accepting Jesus and the truth he has revealed, Jesus' followers accept Jesus' Father. By accepting his Father, Jesus'
followers will somehow share in Jesus' conquest of death.

THE CHURCH'S DIALOGUE WITH TRUTH

The Church, the community of Jesus' followers, is in
constant dialogue with truth. The Church, Jesus' body in
the world, is a community rooted in Word and Sacrament.
The Word, of course, is Jesus. Without going into a detailed and erudite discussion proper to dogmatic theology,
I can apply everything that I have said about truth to the
Church's dialogue with truth.

Truth is the product of a relationship. In the case of the
truth that the Church proclaims, the relationship is between the Church and the Risen Christ. By professing faith
in the Risen Lord, the Church unveils the meaning of life
and death, indeed the meaning of all of history. The
Church's encounter and ongoing dialogue with the Risen
Lord through the centuries have led to the articulation and
development of what Catholics believe. The Nicene Creed

recited at Mass is an example of an articulation by the Church of what she has discovered through her ongoing dialogue with the Risen Lord and her openness to the Holy Spirit.

The Church can unveil the truth of Christian revelation only because she has made a commitment to Jesus. She is his Body. The Church must respond to the Spirit's guidance and is responsible for the truth of revelation that is to be presented and proclaimed in and to the world.

The truth the Church proclaims is essential truth. It is the most radical and basic truth about God, ourselves, and others. Because this truth is so rich, we can always see more deeply into it. Neither we nor the Church in the years to come will exhaust its meaning. As the Church sees more deeply into it, she may articulate it in new ways, though never in ways that will contradict earlier articulations. Truth is dynamic, and the Church is a living community. Her ongoing encounter and dialogue with the Risen Lord and his Spirit will keep her a living sign and source of the truth that saves.

There is no truth more fruitful than the truth that the Church proclaims. The Church's message can lead us into the future in the most effective and important way. The Church proclaims the secret of salvation and the secret of personal existence. She tells us about our Father, about his Risen Son, about the Paraclete sent to teach us and sanctify us. She tells us that by dying to ourselves we will live in a new way. There is no message or meaning presented by any person or institution that can match in beauty or challenge the truth proclaimed by the Church. If we accept it and live it, we will have the most fruitful human lives. We will be saints.

Though the entire Church must proclaim Christian truth, the contemporary priest in a special way is to spread the truth that Jesus has revealed. The Easter event must become real to the priest. The main obligation of the priest is to unveil the truth of the meaning and mystery of Jesus to others and to celebrate that meaning and mystery with others.

All the aspects of truth that were spoken about in this chapter take on a new relevance when applied to the priest's vocation to make Christian truth real to himself and to others.

Christian truth is relational. For it to become real to a person, that individual must open himself or herself to it. If persons do not open themselves to Christian truth, then they must live without it. So each person is responsible for how real Christian truth becomes for him or her. The priest's task is to help people relate to Christian truth and to help them assume responsibility for that truth. As a witness for Jesus, the priest must disturb people's consciousness and conscience and encourage them to root their lives in the most radical truth, Jesus himself.

The priest calls people to make a commitment to the truth. Probably the best way for the priest to call people to make such a commitment is by the evidence of the priest's own commitment to truth. Through his own relationship to Christian truth, the priest is vivified so that he can call others.

Christian truth is the most essential kind of truth because it reveals the most basic meanings about self and God and others. It is also the most fruitful kind of truth because it has the greatest power to change people's lives. The priest has to allow that truth to transform him so that his own life will be a sign to others that Christian truth reveals the most important meanings in the world. The priest must allow the truth to make him free.

IV

PRIESTLY EXISTENCE AND FREEDOM

In terms of popular ideas about freedom, the contemporary priest can seem the epitome of unfreedom. Bound to an authoritarian structure, wearing distinctive garb, not permitted to marry, the priest can seem a relic from another age. However, priestly existence is not only a free existence but the priest by the very meaning of his personhood and his vocation is called to the deepest level of freedom. He also calls others to a deeper freedom.

Today there are two views of freedom that seem especially popular. Each is extreme and neglects the insight of the other. One of these popular views of freedom emphasizes determinism, arguing that freedom is an illusion and that people are programmed in one way or another to act the way they do. B. F. Skinner is probably the most famous proponent of this view. His book *Walden II* is read by many college students in this country. The other popular view is that a free person is one who is totally uninhibited and makes choices arbitrarily based on whim or feeling or whatever. The first view overemphasizes determinism and misses the mystery of freedom; the second view overlooks all the influences—physical, psychological, even previous free choices—that can minimize freedom in any individual life and attributes an almost divine freedom to human beings. Neither view touches very deeply the reality of freedom. What needs emphasis, perhaps especially today, is that freedom means responsibility. To be free is to be responsible for your freedom.

The presence of freedom in personal existence despite all the forces that can influence deterministically is well expressed by Rollo May:

> Freedom and will consist not in the abnegation of determinism but in our *relationship* to it. . . . Man is distinguished by his capacity to know that he is determined, and to choose his relationship to what determines him. He can and must, unless he abdicates his consciousness, choose how he will relate to necessity, such as death, old age, limitations of intelligence, and the conditioning inescapable in his own background. Will he accept this necessity, deny it, fight it, affirm it, consent to it? All these words have an element of volition in them. And it should, by now, be clear that man does not simply "stand outside" in his subjectivity, like a critic at the theater, and look at necessity and decide what he thinks of it. His intentionality is already one element in the necessity in which he finds himself. . . . Intentionality not only makes it possible for us to take a stand vis-à-vis necessity, but requires us to take this stand. This is illustrated *ad infinitum* in psychotherapy, when the patient argues rigid determinism, generally when he is discouraged or wishes to escape the meaning of his intentions. And the more he is "determined to be a

determinist''—the more he argues (which already is intentionality) that he has nothing whatever to do with the fate that is bearing down upon him—the more he is making himself in fact determined.[1]

May's remarks touch upon the most important aspects of freedom that I wish to stress. Because of consciousness, a person can take a stand on all the realities that influence him or her—height, weight, nationality, genetic structure, physical and emotional condition, parents, environment, and so forth. There are numerous influences in a person's life, and most of them underline that a person is not absolutely free. All human freedom is conditional. But none of the influences wipes out freedom as the essence of personal existence.[2] May correctly says that the very fact that a person can take a stand toward what influences him or her, can choose a perspective on what influences him or her, reveals the presence of freedom. Human intentionality—the angle of vision that a person takes—implies freedom. It is precisely conscious freedom that makes personal existence what it is. May says succinctly: ''Man is distinguished by his capacity to know that he is determined, and to choose his relationship to what determines him.'' Conscious freedom is the essence of personal existence. So the primary meaning of freedom as I am discussing it is not the freedom of this act or that act but the radical meaning of personal existence. But I quickly add that if the essence

---

1. Rollo May, *Love and Will* (New York: W. W. Norton, 1969), pp. 269-70.
2. William Luijpen, *Existential Phenomenology* (Pittsburgh: Duquesne University Press, 1969), pp. 186-91, is particularly good on freedom as the essence of personal existence.

of personal existence is conscious freedom, then whatever good human existence does ought to include the increase of freedom. To choose against freedom is to choose against yourself.

SELF-CREATION AND SELF-TRANSCENDENCE

To be a conscious freedom is to be a unique kind of reality. To be conscious freedom is to be a self-creator. It is also to be a self-transcender. Every time a person chooses, he or she creates self. Every free choice is an act by which a person changes self. The more important and serious the choice, the more dramatically the person changes. In the sense that every free choice is a choice of self, every person, the most active and the most passive, the most interested and the most bored, the most dynamic and the least dynamic, is a self-creator.

In discussing the nature of personhood, Bernard Lonergan writes:

> We have now to think of him as a doer, as one that deliberates, evaluates, chooses, acts. Such doing, at first sight, affects, modifies, changes the world of objects. But even more it affects the subject himself. For human doing is free and responsible. Within it is contained the reality of morals, of building up or destroying character, of achieving personality or failing in that task. By his own acts the human subject makes himself what he is to be, and he does so freely and responsibly; indeed, he does so precisely because his acts are the free and responsible experiences of himself.[3]

---

3. Bernard Lonergan, *The Subject* (Milwaukee: Marquette University Press, 1968), p. 19.

Every time a person acts, he or she flings forth his or her being. In each act, a man or woman speaks self.

Because each of us creates self, each person can be described as a self-transcendence. Each time a person acts, he or she goes beyond what he or she was before the action. Each time a person acts, he or she throws himself or herself into the future. Of course, sometimes this action is done in a small way but at other times it is done rather dramatically. Because persons throw themselves into the future, every person can be described as a self-project. The choices that persons make move them in a particular direction. Each person by free choices projects self into the future, and that projection takes a particular direction. Each person's life can be looked on as that individual's project.

Though there are many influences in an individual's life and though in certain areas we may not be as free as we like to think we are, a person is responsible for the project that his or her life is. The basic direction and meaning that an individual's life takes are due to that individual's free choices.

FREEDOM TO CHOOSE

There is a meaning to human existence. In my discussions of a person's horizon and of truth, I emphasized that some horizons and worlds can be very narrow and that others can be expansive. Truth leads us fruitfully into the future while error frustrates us and prevents us from developing. There is a truth to freedom. Some free choices enrich us and deepen our freedom while others do not. While it is true that every person is conscious freedom, it is also true that how a person develops or fails to develop can have an enormous influence on how free that person is in any particular area of activity. Persons can choose against their best interests, against themselves, against their freedom. An obvious example of a person's choosing against freedom would be suicide. Others would be drug or alcohol abuse. Through such choices, persons make themselves less free in a particular area of activity. There are many other examples. Every time persons choose against the meaning of their human nature, they choose unfreedom.

Jean Paul Sartre says a person is condemned to choose. I prefer to say that a person is called to choose. Either way of looking at freedom underlines that there is no way to escape choosing: everyone must choose. But what should and should not be chosen? Even the briefest reflection on freedom raises questions of ethics and morals, the questions that spurred Socrates to state that the unexamined life is not worth living. What is of most interest to us as we reflect on priestly existence are moral choices or choices that free a person to achieve his or her destiny, i.e., choices that most fulfill, deepen, and enrich him or her as a person who is a conscious freedom.

The ten commandments can serve as a good example of rules to guide freedom. Because the commandments are expressed in negative terms, we often think of them as opposed to freedom. But they are guides to a deeper freedom. Adultery works against freedom, lying works against freedom, stealing works against freedom. Sinners are much worse off than the persons against whom they sin. Sinners tie themselves in knots, frustrate themselves, prevent themselves from growing in freedom. In effect, the ten commandments can be partial guides to the richest possible development of freedom. Of course, they are negative guides. The ten commandments tell us what not to do if we wish to be free. In addition to abstaining from certain actions, we must choose certain values. Chastity means more than not committing adultery; honesty means more than not lying or stealing.

Of course, how free any person is depends on that person's world or horizon. If the network of meanings that are real to a person is narrow or shallow, then that person's freedom is going to be restricted. What an individual believes about God, neighbor, and self can either expand his or her freedom or shrink it terribly. Psychiatrist Victor Frankl suggests that an extremely narrow horizon can even lead to neurosis. Discussing the intrinsic religiousness of human nature and his own method of therapy, which Frankl calls logotherapy or meaning therapy, he writes:

> To be sure, it is also a reality that can remain, or again become, unconscious, or be repressed. Precisely in such cases, however, it is the task of logotherapy to re-mind the patient of his unconscious religiousness—that is to say, to let it enter his conscious mind again. After all, it is the business of existential analytic logotherapy to trace the neurotic mode of being to its ultimate ground. Sometimes the ground of neurotic existence is to be seen in a deficiency, in that a person's relation to transcendence is repressed. But although concealed in the "transcendent unconscious," repressed transcendence shows up and makes itself noticeable as an "unrest of the heart." . . . So what holds for the unconscious in general is also true of unconscious religiousness in particular: repression winds up in neurosis.[4]

---

4. Victor E. Frankl, *The Unconscious God: Psychotherapy and Theology* (New York: Simon and Schuster, 1975), pp. 67-68.

So Frankl by his therapeutic approach is trying to help patients extend or expand their horizons or worlds. The broader and more expansive a person's horizon, the greater the opportunities for freedom.

Very much related to a person's freedom and self-project in relation to his or her world or horizon is a person's conscience. We can describe conscience as the habitual way that consciousness judges in moral matters. Just as there are numerous influences on a person's world or horizon, there are numerous influences on an individual's conscience—parents, friends, teachers, schools, literature, film, theatre, the spirit of the age. Once again, however, as with a person's world or horizon, an individual must assume responsibility for his or her conscience.

Conscience plays a key role in shrinking or expanding a world or horizon. Among any group of people, we can find an enormous variation in conscience. One individual's conscience may be very developed in relation to sexual morality but very undeveloped in social matters; another's may be very sensitive in relation to worship but quite undeveloped in relation to truth. Because a person is a dynamic presence to reality, and because a person's world or horizon can change considerably, a person's conscience can undergo dramatic changes.

Archbishop Romero of San Salvador is an example. Apparently, before he became the ordinary of the diocese, his social conscience was largely undeveloped. However, he soon became a champion of the rights of the poor and downtrodden. His social conscience and freedom eventually led to his martyrdom.[5]

FREEDOM'S PURPOSE

A person can and does transcend self. But is there any goal to this transcendence, any direction to it, any purpose to it? This question is crucial in relation to freedom because if there is no purpose and goal for transcendence, then freedom seems absurd. Rather than a gift from God, it becomes some kind of mistake in the evolutionary process, a mistake that we are condemned to employ. This view was adopted by atheistic existentialist Sartre. What Sartre saw clearly was that freedom, if it has any purpose, demands the existence of God. But Sartre believed there was no God; so to him freedom became a terrible absurdity. Sartre's plays *No Exit* and *The Flies* provide excellent dramatization of his view of freedom and also of his atheism.

In *No Exit* Sartre places two women and a man in hell. They cannot relate in any way that promotes their freedom. Each is an obstacle to freedom for the others. At one point one woman in a fit of rage says to the male character, Garcin:

> Ah, wasn't I right when I said you were vulnerable?
> Now you're going to pay the price, and what a price!
> You're a coward, Garcin, because I wish it. I wish
> it—do you hear?—I wish it. And yet, just look at me,

---

5. Archbishop Romero is not Catholicism's only recent martyr. There have been many in Latin America. See Penny Lernoux, *Cry of the People* (New York: Doubleday, 1980), a fine book about the Church's role in Latin America.

> see how weak I am, a mere breath on the air, a gaze
> observing you, a formless thought that thinks you.[6]

Her vision of him will lock him in, will prevent him from growing and developing freely. She will shrink his world, narrow his horizon. He will be at her mercy. Thus the significance of the most famous line in the play: "Hell is other people." In Sartre's view, people prevent one another from being free.

The Flies is a classic example of contemporary atheism. From Marx and Nietzsche through Freud and Sartre, just about every atheist in the last one hundred years has been unable to conceive of a God who does not rob humankind of freedom.[7] In a conversation between the god Zeus and the rebel Orestes, Zeus reminds the upstart that he is god and that he rules the universe. Orestes replies:

> . . . Your whole universe is not enough to prove me wrong. You are the king of gods, king of stones and stars, king of the waves of the sea. But you are not the king of man.
>
> Zeus: Impudent spawn! So I am not your king? Who, then, made you?
>
> Orestes: You. But you blundered; you should not have made me free.
>
> Zeus: I gave you freedom so that you might serve me.

---

6. Jean Paul Sartre, *No Exit* in *No Exit and Three Other Plays* (New York: Vantage Books, 1946), p. 45.
7. See Henri De Lubac, *The Drama of Atheist Humanism*, trans. Edith M. Riley (New York: Meridian, 1963), an especially good presentation of nineteenth century atheism.

Orestes: Perhaps. But now it has turned against its giver. And neither you nor I can undo what has been done.

Zeus: Ah, at last! So this is your excuse?

Orestes: I am not excusing myself.

Zeus: No? Let me tell you it sounds much like an excuse, this freedom whose slave you claim to be.

Orestes: Neither slave nor master. I am my freedom. No sooner had you created me than I ceased to be yours.[8]

In examining a priest's freedom, I am promoting a view directly opposed to that of Sartre: I believe that people can free one another and that a relationship with God can be the most freeing reality. Sartre was right to insist that the human heart demands God. In a poignant section of his autobiography, *The Words*, Sartre writes:

> I have just related the story of a missed vocation. I needed God, He was given to me, I received Him without realizing that I was seeking Him. Failing to take root in my heart, He vegetated in me for a while, then He died. Whenever anyone speaks to me about Him today, I say with the easy amusement of an old beau who meets a former belle: "Fifty years ago, had it not been for that misunderstanding, that mistake, the accident that separated us, there might have been something between us!"[9]

Christians believe that there is a God who corresponds to the human heart's deepest longing. Commitment to God

---

8. Sartre, *The Flies* in *No Exit and Three Other Plays,* pp. 120-21.

9. Jean Paul Sartre, *The Words*, trans. Bernard Frechtman (New York: Fawcett, 1966), pp. 64-65.

and loving friendship with God are freedom's deepest reason, purpose, and goal.

A PRIEST'S FREEDOM

A priest's existence is rooted in Christian freedom. Like every person, a priest is a self-creator and a self-transcender. However, priestly existence affords extraordinary possibilities for self-creation and self-transcendence. The reason is the priest's proximity to God's Word and Sacrament.

The type of self-creation and self-transcendence to which a priest is called is beautifully expressed in Jesuit Gerard Manley Hopkins's poem #34. Hopkins writes about how the nature of each thing speaks itself, throws forth its being, speaks its essence, reveals its depth. Each creature has its own nature, and in Hopkins's vision of reality:

> Each mortal thing does one thing and the same:
> Deals out that being indoors each one dwells;
> Selves—goes itself, myself it speaks and spells.

When he speaks of man in grace, Hopkins says that such a man speaks more—he speaks Christ. Hopkins writes:

> I say more: the just man justices;
> Keeps grace: that keeps all his goings graces;
> Acts in God's eye what in God's eye he is—
> Christ—for Christ plays in ten thousand places,
> Lovely in limbs, and lovely in eyes not his
> To the Father through the features of man's faces.[10]

The priest is called to direct his self-creativity and his self-transcendence so that he can become like Christ. The

---

10. *Gerard Manley Hopkins: Selection of His Poems,* ed. W. H. Gardner (London: Penguin, 1953), p. 51.

life of a priest is a life that is centered on God's Word. The truth of God's Word calls the priest to a deeper freedom. In any dialogue, a person can be called to a deeper freedom. All truth is fruitful; so all truth leads toward freedom rather than toward frustration. But the dialogue between a priest and God's Word holds out special opportunities for a priest to transcend himself. Discussing dialogue, theologian Gregory Baum writes:

> From the beginning, then, there are moments when the word addressed to us makes us abandon the world of our own making and enter upon a new life. Dialogue is not simply a way of giving and receiving information, it does not change man simply by expanding his knowledge. Again and again as we are in dialogue with others, we must hear the painful word which overcomes us and evokes a response in us that transforms life. The word addressed to us at those moments reveals to us the truth of which we are afraid. It pierces the screen we have erected between ourselves and reality. Then we must either flee from this word and hide more effectively behind our defenses, or open ourselves to it, go through the painful passage from superficiality to greater depth, and receive the truth that has been uttered to us. Sometimes dialogue is a happy sharing, but in the course of a man's life there are those important yet frequent moments when dialogue means conversion. Because we have listened, because we were willing to let go the little world of our own making, because we have gained a new hold on reality, we have come to be person in a new way. Our response to the word addressed to us has been constitutive of who we are.[11]

---

11. Gregory Baum, *Man Becoming* (New York: Herder and Herder, 1970), p. 43.

The priest's exposure to God's Word affords him special opportunities to respond, "to be person in a new way." He is constantly being called to go beyond where he is. He is being called to create his future with Christ, which is another way of saying to create himself with Christ.

A contemporary myth, and one whose falsity has tremendous power to harm, is that we increase our freedom by refraining from all commitments. A superficial understanding of personal existence suggests that a commitment ties us up, binds us, restricts us, and so the best way to remain free and increase our freedom is to abstain from all commitments and especially from any life commitment. In a provocative essay entitled "Creative Fidelity," Catholic existentialist philosopher Gabriel Marcel exposes the poverty of this type of thinking.[12] Marcel points out that we tend to think of the future as something external to ourselves that happens to us. We tend to think of the future like the weather—a reality over which we have no control. Marcel emphasizes that we create our future. We do so chiefly through our commitments. The very nature of personal existence, the very nature of a conscious freedom, requires that for it to be fulfilled it must be given away. In his writings, Marcel analyzes such activities as hope, fidelity, and love and concludes that it is only through commitment that freedom can reach its fulfillment. Though we are not in complete control of the future in the sense that we control all the events that will happen, we are in control of who we are and who we will be because we are free. We are

---

12. Gabriel Marcel, "Creative Fidelity" in *Creative Fidelity*, trans. Robert Rosthal (New York: Farrar, Straus & Giroux, 1964), pp. 147-74.

responsible for our self-project. By making a loving commitment, we can achieve a level of personhood that cannot be reached in any other way. Of course, to what or to whom the commitment is made is crucial.

Every Gospel scene suggests the freedom of Jesus. He is the man for others. The self-project of Jesus is service of his fellow human beings and service of his Father. This commitment to service liberates Jesus. However, before his resurrection he is limited by time and space. The resurrection liberates Jesus totally. Now he can be lovingly present to everyone in every place.

The priest's self-project is an imitation of Jesus. Sharing through grace in Jesus' risen presence, the priest tries to be present in loving service to others. He tries to be faithful, to be present not only to others but for others. A priest's commitment is to service of God and people. Through loving presence to God and people, a priest will allow the deepest, most exciting, and most liberating world and horizon to open up to him. By being open throughout his life to God's Word, a priest will allow his conscience to be sensitized. He will, in the words of St. Paul, let that mind be in him which was in Christ Jesus.

Of course, one of the key ways that a priest achieves his own freedom is through calling others to freedom. He calls others to open themselves to the Word that liberates. He calls others to transcend themselves in conversion. He calls others to the experience of the first followers of Jesus, an experience of being liberated from sin and evil. The popular image of Christianity as opposed to freedom could not be further from the truth. In *The Conspiracy of God*, John Haughey writes about the Pentecost experience of the apostles.

Pentecost was a jail break! What had bound them was now loosened. Their dancing feet, marveling tongues and exuberant hearts were the evidence that bound men were now free. Free from what? From the images that they had entertained about themselves.

Or, to change the metaphor, Pentecost was the moment in which the new Breath which was breathed into them drove out all the poisonous fumes of negative self-images they had unwittingly inhaled from their milieu and each other. There is considerable evidence in the Gospels of the apostles' attitude toward themselves. Their anxiety, for example, about who was to be the greatest in the Kingdom that was being established was not naked ambition but the need to cover over personal disesteem by position. . . . The joy of the Kingdom belongs to those to whom it has been given to inhale the truth about themselves. The limitations that are imposed by each baptized Christian on the power of the Spirit that would operate new pentecosts in each of us come not so much from our sinfulness, I suspect, as from an unwillingness to entertain the view of ourselves that God has of us. The Spirit's power in us is meant to provide an alternative to self-definitions that are fallacious and, consequently, unfreeing.[13]

A priest is a pentecost person. He tries to participate in the freedom that Pentecost brought and to call others to participate in that freedom.

---

13. John Haughey, *The Conspiracy of God* (Garden City, N.Y.: Doubleday, 1973), pp. 92-93.

V

THE PRIEST: A COMMUNITY PERSON

In exploring both the problems that beset priestly existence and the challenge present within priestly existence,
two concepts used by contemporary existentialists can be
especially helpful. They are facticity and subjectivity.
Though they can seem rather technical, their meaning is
relatively clear and, in terms of understanding the meaning
of personal existence, their importance cannot be exces-
sively emphasized. Every person is a combination of facticity and subjectivity.

Facticity refers to all the facts about a person, all the
determinations of a person—the height, weight, nationality, sexuality, I.Q., skin color, and so forth. New facts and
determinations are being added to a person all the time.
Though the list of determinations of any given individual
would be endless, at least facts can be listed; they can be
named. If I were to use my best friend as an example, I
could name numerous facts or determinations about him.

Subjectivity is more mysterious. It refers to the center or core of a person. It refers to the particular unique conscious freedom that this individual person is. It refers to that unique center, that unrepeatable conscious freedom, that special irreplaceable mysterious personal center whom God created. There are no words to capture subjectivity. While I could write hundreds of words articulating the facts about my best friend, there is no word or set of words that would capture his subjectivity. Most words are general and universal, and my best friend is unique. Even his name will not solve the problem because there are a million men with his name. Because this uniqueness is difficult if not impossible to articulate, it is easy for us to overlook it or to reduce it to something else. This problem is a key issue in contemporary society. We tend to reduce people to their facticity. We reduce them to one or more of their determinations.

A friend of mine recently provided me with a frightening illustration of how a person can be reduced to his determinations. My friend is in medical school. One day while a group of medical students was being led by one of the professors through the wards they came upon a patient, a small boy about ten days old who had a hole in the top of his head. By looking into the hole much of his brain could be observed. The boy did not have long to live, and, of course, his parents were heartbroken. Later in the day at lunch my friend almost became nauseous as he listened to two of his classmates elatedly discuss how "fascinating" it was to look inside the head. They spoke of the boy as though he were an interesting machine. They had reduced the boy to his facticity. He was no longer a human being in a tragic situation. He was an object to study.

I describe this phenomenon of reducing people to their facticity as the "nothing but" approach. We single out some fact or determination of some individual and then treat the person as though he or she were nothing but this quality or qualities. We treat an individual as though she were nothing but a housewife or as though he were nothing but a janitor or as though she were nothing but a secretary or as though he were nothing but a clerk. We reduce a person to his or her facticity and overlook the individual's subjectivity. We reduce a person to some quality or attribute or role. This kind of reduction can take place in any human relationship. For example, it can happen between a teacher and a student, between a priest and a parishioner, between a doctor and a patient. I am not suggesting that every human relationship must become a close friendship. This expectation would put impossible burdens on people. But I am suggesting that because no person is identical with his or her facticity, no person in any relationship should be reduced to "nothing but" his or her facticity. To do so to anyone is to reduce the person to a thing.

PRESSURES TO REDUCE PERSONS TO THINGS

There are all sorts of reasons why this problem is most common today. We live at a fast pace. Everyone seems to be rushing somewhere. As the little boy points out in Antoine Saint-Exupery's wisdom-filled book, *The Little Prince*, we do not appear to have time to pause over people. We are under all sorts of pressures, not the least of which is economic. Just making a living, just achieving a human level of existence in our society, has become such a task that people do not seem to have the luxury of relating in any depth.

The media seem to encourage us to relate to one another on the level of facticity. Check any commercial on television and you will probably discover that its message can be translated into: "Your present facticity makes you unlovable. Change your facticity by buying our product, and you will become lovable." That seems to be the message, whether the product is toothpaste or slacks, deodorants or jeans. Of course, there is a double error in the message. The first error is that we are unlovable because of our facticity. Not possible. There is no such reality as an unlovable person. Even if he wanted to, God could not make an unlovable person. An unlovable person is a square circle. To be a person is to be lovable. The second error is that by changing our facticity we will become lovable. Not so. We are lovable because of *who* we are, not because of any facts or determinations about us. By identifying ourselves with our facticity or by allowing others to identify us with our facticity, we allow ourselves to be reduced to a thing. We allow our uniqueness or subjectivity to be overlooked.

One of the more serious problems in our society is that we spend more and more time with people we never meet deeply. Today more and more people seem to feel the need for community. So many of their relationships are superficial that people seem to be starving for community. The popularity of marriage encounter weekends, teenage "awakenings," *cursillos*, prayer groups is just one sign of people's need for more intimacy in their relationships. One reason why a prayer group meeting can go on for three or four hours is that people are experiencing one another on a level far more intimate and profound than the superficial relationships that characteristize their day-to-day lives.

The pressures to deal with one another as though we are nothing but facticity are strong. When individuals succumb, both partners in the relationship suffer. If a man reduces a woman to nothing but a sex object, it is not only the woman whose subjectivity is overlooked. The man, by approaching her this way and locking her into some role, at the same time locks himself into a role. If she is nothing but a sex object, then he is nothing but a man who leers at sex objects. To see the danger in this reduction, we have to realize that it is happening throughout society. People are not approaching and relating as persons but in terms of their power, status, physical appearance, and income. To identify persons with any of these facts is to reduce them to something less than themselves. To relate to them totally in terms of one of these is to reduce ourselves to something less than ourselves.

I wonder how influential *Playboy* is. It sells millions of copies in this country. Apparently some American males are buying its philosophy of life and its view of women. Even those who do not consciously accept the *Playboy* philosophy or its view of women may be influenced by the vision it promotes. The narcissism in the *Playboy* philosophy encourages the male playboy to use people. Anyone who embraces this narcissistic view will tend to use people, to reduce them to the role that would best serve the user.

LONELINESS AND COEXISTENCE

A society whose members reduce one another to facticity is a lonely society. I see loneliness as a feeling of being insignificant, a feeling of not mattering to anyone, a feeling of being unimportant to anyone, a feeling of being unloved by anyone. Everyone experiences loneliness at some time in his or her life. Loneliness can even be looked upon as a call to growth.[1] However, in a society in which much emphasis is put on status and power, loneliness can be almost unbearable. In the secular society in which he tries to preach the Gospel of Christ, the contemporary priest can be particularly vulnerable to feelings of loneliness.[2] He can feel that he is insignificant, unimportant, and of no special value to his contemporaries.

In order to capture the implications of people's personhood being reduced to facticity, we need to call attention to a radical truth about personal existence: a person does not just exist but coexists. Personal existence demands community with other persons. Referring to a human person as an "existent," theologian John Macquarrie writes the following about the coexistence of persons:

> That community belongs to the essential or primordial constitution of the existent may be established in various ways. . . . For although each person has his own unique perspective on the world, the very notion of "world" implies a common world. This is very clear, for instance, in the conception of an instrumental world. We have noted that no instrument can be understood in complete isolation—it implies all kinds of other instruments and materials, and the context of tasks in which these are used. But equally the instrumental world implies other existents. The typewriter I use implies not just the paper on which to type and the machinery that produced the type-

---

1. In my book *Loneliness Is For Loving* (Notre Dame, Ind.: Ave Maria Press, 1978), I examine loneliness and suggest that it can be used as a call to love.
2. I developed this idea in "Ministry in a Secularized World," *Emmanuel* 86 (May 1980): 261-66.

writer, but also the people who designed, produced and marketed the typewriter, and the people who are going to read what I type on the paper. The everyday world, then, is already a world that implies an indefinite number of people engaged in interlocking and mutually supportive tasks.[3]

On every level of human existence, an individual needs others in order to be a person. Obviously, a person needs others physically: a child receives life, nourishment, and lodging from his or her parents. However, our coexistence goes beyond the physical. We coexist intellectually, emotionally, and spiritually.

I can write this book only because some brilliant existentialist philosophers wrote books that I was given the opportunity to study by my bishop. You can read this book only because publishers took all the steps necessary to get it into print. From the moment we were able to listen to our parents, we have coexisted intellectually. Our parents gave us a whole world of meaning. In grammar school, high school, college, and beyond we depend on others' insights, information, and interest. Every day as I hold the *New York Times* in my hand, if I reflect on the number of people whose efforts made that newspaper available to me, I realize how I coexist with others concerning knowledge. Any time I watch a television newscast, I coexist with those who have investigated the world and decided what is and what is not news. In New York there is a radio station that broadcasts the news all day long. The theme spoken again and again during the day by one of the station's an-

---

3. John Macquarrie, *Existentialism* (London: Penguin, 1973), p. 77.

nouncers is: "You give us twenty-two minutes, and we'll give you the world." I am very aware that I coexist with others when I hear that the news of the entire world is going to be handed to me every twenty-two minutes.

INTELLECTUAL COEXISTENCE

When I was newly ordained over twenty years ago, I organized a priests' discussion group. The group was an excellent example of how people coexist intellectually. We—about fifteen of us—met one night a month. Each month we chose some book in theology to read and discuss. We shared insights and problems. Occasionally, we would invite a professional theologian to lead the discussion. The group lasted four years. I believe every member of that group would look back on those discussions as both highly informative and strongly formative experiences.

Jewish theologian Abraham Heschel underlined that we coexist intellectually especially in our pursuit of the most important meanings. He writes:

> Man in his being is derived from, attended by, and directed to the being of community. For man *to be* means *to be with* other human beings. His existence is coexistence. He can never attain fulfilment, or sense meaning, unless it is shared, unless it pertains to other human beings.
>
> Although it is true that in order to grasp the meaning of being human we analyze the human individual rather than the human species, any analysis that disregards social involvement, man's interdependence and correlativity, will miss the heart of being human.
>
> Human solidarity is not the product of being human; being human is the product of human solidarity. Indeed, even the most personal concern, the search for meaning, is utterly meaningless as a pur-

suit of personal salvation. Its integrity discloses compassion, a hope or intuition of meaning in which all men may share.[4]

EMOTIONAL COEXISTENCE

I also coexist emotionally. This coexistence probably began in my mother's womb. My coexistence with my parents was certainly important in my early years. The children in my neighborhood, the teachers I had throughout my schooling, my fellow seminarians, the priests with whom I have worked and lived have all contributed to my emotional make-up. Wherever we are, we coexist emotionally.

I have discovered that when I visit people's homes I can notice an emotional atmosphere. There are homes in which I can detect the joy and good feeling that the members of the family share with one another. I can sense that the atmosphere is filled with good vibrations. There are other homes in which the hostility within the family is so strong that I just hope I can get out alive.

An experience that was repeated a couple of times in my life can underline how we coexist emotionally. For a couple of years, one of my closest friends was stationed with me at the college seminary where I teach. Often I would visit his room late at night, and we would discuss our apostolate to the college seminarians. My friend was an optimistic priest. He was enthused about his work, about the liturgical changes, about the latest statements from the pope. His approach to everything in the contemporary

---

4. Abraham Heschel, *Who Is Man?* (Palo Alto, Calif.: Stanford University Press, 1965), p. 45.

Church was optimistic and joyful. Occasionally, when I would leave his room and return to my own room, my phone would ring. It would be a classmate who was also a close friend. My classmate would talk about the same topics that my fellow professor had talked about, but my classmate would be negative and sad. It was a strange experience for me. I wondered if I were living in two different churches. What would happen if I coexisted only with people like my professor friend? I imagine I might become Pollyanna and miss some of the real problems in the Church. What would happen if I coexisted only with people like my classmate? One evening I had an insight into what that might be like. My classmate once asked me to cover him for confessions. After the afternoon confessions, I had dinner in the rectory. I could not believe the atmosphere. The outlook of the priests on everything in the post-Vatican II Church seemed negative. The dinner was a devastating experience for me. After I left, I wondered what it must be like to have dinner there every evening. I had dinner there once and was affected by the negative atmosphere. My classmate was there every evening. Such an atmosphere has to take its toll. For better or worse, we coexist emotionally.

The spiritual director at the seminary at which I studied frequently used the term "Archie" in his talks to the student body. By the term, he meant to indicate the person we liked least, the person who most annoyed us. Our "Archie" was the person we found most difficult to love. We found the expression rather humorous. In jest, seminarians would ask one another, "How's your Archie?" It was only years later after experiencing members of different communities that I began to see why the spiritual director emphasized how persons should relate to their "Archies." We coexist emotionally. One person in a community, if he acts as "Archie" for many or even for a few, can have a devastating effect on the community. An abrasive personality, a hostile individual, a person with severe changes of mood can wreak havoc in a community. If permitted, he or she can destroy a community. Just the awareness that we coexist emotionally can help to free someone from the deleterious influence of another's internal problem.

SPIRITUAL COEXISTENCE

We also coexist spiritually. God has decided to deal with us as a community. We are not saved as individuals but as brothers and sisters in Christ. Of course, no one can substitute for my freedom; nor can anyone stand in my place before God. Jesus has won redemption for us, and each of us must respond to God's grace. Yet we can have a profound influence on one another's spiritual lives. The faith of someone else can have a profound influence on my faith. The hope that animates someone's life can call me to hope. The love for Jesus that drives someone to be interested in others can inspire me to a greater love and unselfishness.

I suppose no doctrine in Catholicism so calls attention to the truth that we coexist spiritually as the doctrine of the Mystical Body or the doctrine of the People of God. There are invisible bonds tying us together. While the Church is perfectly holy in its head Jesus, the holiness of its members changes during different periods of history. If the priest who preaches to the congregation every week is a saint, then that congregation has a tremendous opportunity to grow in holiness. If the preacher has lost his faith, then the congregation's faith will probably suffer, at least in the sense that it will not be challenged. If as a priest I am living with a community of priests who are prayerful, dedicated men, I will be called to deeper Christian living. I will not be called or challenged by a community of men who are lazy and selfish.

That people coexist spiritually was dramatically and disturbingly depicted in Graham Greene's play *The Living Room*. One of the key characters in the play is an invalid priest confined to a wheelchair. The priest lives with his two maiden sisters. In the house they inhabit, a number of rooms have been closed off because members of the family have died in them. The two sisters are afraid of death. At the climax of the play, the priest's niece, who has been having an affair with a psychologist who is a married man, comes to the priest for help. Over the last twenty years, the priest has not been a man of prayer. When the priest tries but fails to help, his niece commits suicide. Disclosing his conversation with his niece to the psychologist, the priest says:

> For more than twenty years I've been a useless priest. I had a real vocation for the priesthood—perhaps you'd explain it in terms of a father complex. Never mind now, I'm not laughing at you. To me it was a real vocation. And for twenty years it's been imprisoned in this chair—the desire to help. You have it too in your own way, and it would still be there if you lost your sight and speech. Last night God gave me a chance. He flung this child at my knees, asking for help, asking for hope. That's what she said, "Can't you give me anything to hope for?" I said to God, "Put words into my mouth"; but he's

given me twenty years in this chair with nothing to do but prepare for such a moment, so why should he interfere? And all I said was "You can pray." If I'd ever really known what prayer was I would only have had to touch her to give her peace.[5]

We coexist spiritually. Because the priest was not able to give his niece something for which to hope, she committed suicide. Though every person is responsible for his or her free response to or rejection of God's grace, we can and do influence one another.

Coexistence in spirituality is a special kind of coexistence. In most other ways of coexisting, with the exception of love (and coexistence in love is deeply related to coexistence in spirituality), we are changed on the level of facticity by others, i.e., we are *made* by others, or we receive new determination through others. William Luijpen explains:

Man makes *man* be. For this reason we must say that "this" man is a New Yorker through New Yorkers, a smoker through smokers, a philosopher through philosophers, a Christian through Christians. Similarly, a mother is a mother through her children; a sick person is really sick only when he is visited or forgotten; a Negro is really a Negro when Whitey refuses to admit him to his bowling alley or closes the doors of the university to him; an asocial family is really asocial only when other families want to have nothing to do with them, or when a social worker comes for a visit; a cute little button nose is really a cute little button

---

5. Graham Greene, *The Living Room* (London: William Heinemann Ltd., 1953), pp. 63-64.

> nose only when others notice it; a baldhead is a real
> baldhead only when he is called that by others.[6]

In the secular society in which he coexists, a priest must be careful what he allows others to make him be. Because a person is conscious freedom, none of this "making be" happens automatically. There are enormous pressures that can have a powerful influence on an individual, but they never influence a person as though he or she were only a thing.

AUTHENTIC AND INAUTHENTIC COMMUNITY

Because the very nature of personal existence is coexistence, the groups to which an individual belongs become very important. There are authentic communities and inauthentic communities. Referring to personal being as "existence," Macquarrie observes:

> What is the criterion by which one distinguishes an
> authentic from an inauthentic being-with-others?
> Authentic being-with-others is precisely that mode of
> relation to the other that promotes existence in the
> full sense; that is to say, it lets the human stand out as
> human, in freedom and responsibility. On the other
> hand, inauthentic being-with-others suppresses the
> genuinely human and personal. Whatever kind of
> relation to the others depersonalizes and dehuman-
> izes is an inauthentic one. Thus there is a paradox in-
> volved here. A purely individual existence is not
> possible and could not properly be called an "ex-
> istence"; yet existence with the others is to be judged
> authentic to the degree that it lets individuals be free

---

6. William Luijpen, *Existential Phenomenology* (Pittsburgh: Duquesne University Press, 1969), p. 267.

to become the unique persons that they are. True community allows for true diversity.[7]

Noting that in an inauthentic community uniformity is imposed, Macquarrie continues:

> At the everyday level of relations between persons, no doubt much so-called community is of the inauthentic kind. It is simply the crowd, the herd, the mass, the they, or whatever one may wish to call it. It is the pressure toward uniformity, which has been enormously heightened in modern times by the mass media of communication and the mass products unloaded upon a consumer society. . ... . Perhaps it is only by breaking out of a distorted being-with-others that the possibility of building a genuine community can arise. One might compare the "black power" phase in the struggle of the American Negro toward full citizenship. An oppressive relationship has to be broken and a sense of independence and dignity enjoyed before an affirmative and genuine relation can be built up.[8]

Because a priest's vocation is unique, he has to be especially careful about the groups to which he belongs. The large group or community that we have described as the secular society will not be of much help to him. Besides embracing a vision of life that is quite different from a priest's vision of life, contemporary society may have become so thing-oriented that it does not encourage its members to coexist in that unique way we call love.

> In society, as in the spiritual world, secular goals have come to predominate; the national organization of the economy has increased human power over na-

---

7. Macquarrie, p. 91.
8. Ibid., p. 92.

ture, and politically also society has become more rational, utilitarian, democratic, with a resulting material wealth and progress. The men of the Enlightenment foresaw no end to this triumphant expansion of reason into all the areas of social life. But here too reason has foundered upon its opposite, upon the absurd and unpredictable realities—wars, economic crises and dislocations, political upheavals among the masses. Moreover, man's feeling of homelessness, of alienation has been intensified in the midst of a bureaucratized, impersonal mass society. He has come to feel himself an outsider even within his own human society. He is trebly alienated: a stranger to God, to nature, and to the gigantic social apparatus that supplies his material wants.

But the worst and final form of alienation, toward which indeed the others tend, is man's alienation from his own self. In a society that requires of man only that he perform competently his own particular social function, man becomes identified with this function, and the rest of his being is allowed to subsist as best it can—usually to be dropped below the surface of consciousness and forgotten.[9]

During the last couple of years, in addition to teaching philosophy at the college seminary, I have been the school's director of public relations. For the most part, this job requires me to visit high schools trying to promote the college seminary so that young men who think they might have a vocation to the priesthood would consider attending this school. The first year I had the job I made about twenty to twenty-five visits to high schools. What I suspected before I started, I became more convinced of as I

---

9. William Barrett, *Irrational Man* (Garden City, N.Y.: Doubleday Anchor Book, 1962), pp. 35-36.

made my rounds. There is almost nothing in our society encouraging a young man to be a priest. The values that the society promotes are almost the exact opposite of the values that a priest who is trying to imitate Jesus ought to embrace. My initial reaction as I visited high schools was discouragement as I found such a minimal response. However, as I reflected on the pressures working against high school students choosing the priesthood, I was amazed that anyone wanted to be a priest. Even the minimal response that I observed seemed to be a miracle of grace. If there is little in society that encourages or supports a young man's decision to be a priest, then there is little that supports a man's decision to continue to be a priest or to grow in priestly existence.

ENTERING THE CHRISTIAN COMMUNITY

To be a person, to be a personal existence, is to be a conscious bodiliness in the world. A person's horizon or world is a network of meanings that are real to an individual. In other ages, the world or horizon of many people was Christian. Not so today. The contemporary priest functions in a post-Christian world. This reality puts special pressure on both him and those to whom he is ministering. No one can be a person alone. I cannot be me without you; you cannot be you without me. For better or worse, we need one another. We will influence one another. The crucial question is: how will we influence one another? Will we influence one another for better or worse? The answer for the believer is to enter as deeply as possible into the Christian community. The contemporary priest must experience Christian community in at least two ways: he must help to form a Christian community as part of his apostolate, and he must be part of a community if he is to grow or perhaps even survive as a Christian minister. In a Christian community, persons try to coexist precisely as Christians. The community is rooted in truth and love, and its members try to serve one another in these two areas.

Christian community is rooted in the Word. In an atmosphere pervaded by all sorts of meanings, the Christian community bases itself on a special set of meanings. These meanings provide its vision, its basis, and its nourishment. There are no meanings more exciting and inspiring than Christian meanings. While it is easy to recite Christian meanings in a creed, it is less easy to allow them to become the center of one's horizon and one's world. Today it is not easy to allow Christian meanings to be the most real meanings in life. Hence a community rooted in these meanings becomes especially important today.

Members of the Christian community try to unveil Christian truth for one another. The truth that provides the meaning by which Christians live, the vision that Christians embrace, was first unveiled in the birth, life, death, and resurrection of Jesus. Christ's human existence was the primary event by which truth was unveiled. In the Christ-event, the meaning of God and the meaning of personal existence were especially unveiled. In the Risen Christ is the truth about God and human persons. This truth was unveiled for Jesus' followers by Jesus' Spirit, the Spirit of Truth. The meaning of the Christ-event is still being unveiled by the Holy Spirit to Jesus' followers today. The Spirit of Truth is the soul of the Christian community and to that community the Spirit is still unveiling the meaning of the Christ-event.

One of the most important ways that the Spirit unveils the truth to the community is through the pope and bishops. Besides being guided by the Spirit not to teach error to the entire community, the pope and bishops, through their teachings, are to lead the community more deeply into the truth. Studying the community's history, we discover that at some periods of time the pope and bishops did so better than at others. We also learn that they made some of the implications of the Christ-event more clear than others. Because all truth is dynamic and developing, the community and its leaders, the pope and bishops, can see more and more clearly into the meaning of the Christ-event. The impetus for new insight need not always come from the top. The community coexists in truth, and so there have been and will be others who call the community to new insights.

Some of these others might have been the theologians and prophets. Each has a special role in the community. The theologian prayerfully explores God's Word and tries to clarify its meaning for the community. In recent years, the community has come to appreciate the role of the theologian more. In a special sense, he is a teacher in the Church. His insights and reflections can contribute toward making the community more open and more committed to the truth. Throughout the history of the community, there have been prophets. They can call the community's attention to some neglected or forgotten aspect of the Christ-event or to some new implication of that event.

Because the community coexists in truth, everyone is called upon to teach Christian truth in some way even if it is only by the good example of a life based on that truth. But given the present structure of the Church, the priest has a special role in unveiling truth to the community. On the local scene, he is the official spokesman. The community has sent him away for special study. It has provided him with the freedom to perceive and reflect on truth so that he might serve the community by helping it to embrace the truth more strongly and live it more ardently.

Even in our age of the media, for many Catholics Christian truth is filtered through the local priest. Whatever the pope and bishops teach, whatever the theologians and prophets are saying, the local priest has a unique opportunity to unveil Christian truth to the community. Within his area of the vineyard, no one else has either the opportunity or the obligation that he has to make Christian truth relevant. Depending on how real and exciting Christian truth is to the priest, he will make it real and exciting to his community. He will do so through his homilies but also through all the teaching opportunities that are available to him in the local community. Whether he is teaching in the pulpit, the rectory office, or the classroom, the priest is trying to unveil truth, open up a new world for people, and help them extend and expand their horizons.

REACHING OUT TO PEOPLE IN THEIR SUBJECTIVITY

The Christian community is rooted in love. The model of a life of love and service for the Christian is Jesus. We can look in vain through the Gospel scenes to find Jesus reducing some person to his or her facticity. Jesus never does that. He never takes a "nothing but" approach to people. Jesus always approaches people on the level of their subjectivity. He reaches out to their uniqueness, to their singularity, to the mystery of their selves. In each Gospel scene, Jesus seems to be ready to establish what some philosophers have called an I-Thou relationship. He at the center of his person is ready to meet others at the center of their person. Jesus clearly is a man for others.

When in the Gospel people open themselves to Jesus, their lives often change dramatically. One thinks of the apostles at a few words from Jesus leaving their families and jobs. We know from our own experience that, in any I-Thou encounter, striking changes can occur in the persons involved. This change seems to happen time and again to people who encounter Jesus.

In every encounter Jesus has with someone in the Gospel, Jesus basically is doing the same thing: he is calling the person to open himself or herself to Jesus' Father. Jesus is calling the person to say a loving "yes" to the Father's self-gift. I think it is legitimate to say that prior to his death Jesus' ability to call people to open themselves to his Father's self-gift was to some extent limited. What I mean is that Jesus, prior to his death, could be in only one place at a time and only with a limited group of people. We can tell from the Gospel scenes that even prior to his death Jesus had a special presence, that he was so free that he was able to be present to people in a very affirming, supportive, and liberating manner. But after the love-explosion of the resurrection, Jesus is present not only in one place to a limited group but everywhere to all persons. The Risen Jesus through his loving presence is still calling people to open themselves to his Father's self-gift. Jesus makes this call not only through his individual presence but through the community of his followers, the Easter community, whose meaning and mission are centered on the Risen Lord. In as many ways as possible, the community, in imitation of Jesus, reaches out in love toward the subjectivity of people.

The priest tries to be a person who never approaches people with a "nothing but" attitude. He tries never to reduce people to their facticity. He also tries to keep before the members of the community the meaning and mission of the community. If the Christian community is not a community of love, it is nothing. It must be a community of loving service if it is going to imitate its head. Whatever projects the community embraces, they ultimately must be for the benefit of people. By his own love and concern for people, the priest can call others to loving service. More than any other group, the Christian community focuses on the subjectivity of its members. Those members are called to serve the subjectivity of one another and of those who do not belong to the community. The nature of the Christian community is to be a love community. Crucial to the meaning of a priest's coexistence is the meaning of love.

VI

LOVE AND PRIESTLY EXISTENCE

Since Vatican II there has been an enormous emphasis on the role that love plays in religion—indeed to some it seems like a gross overemphasis. On all levels of teaching religion, from grammar school to theological graduate school, theories and insights connected with love have been propounded. Some have felt that they were discovering something new, others that they were returning to previous insights that had been neglected. Coupled with the tremendous emphasis in our society on heterosexual interpersonal love, the emphasis within the Catholic community can seem to make the life of a celibate priest less than meaningful. I suggest that the opposite is true: that the life of a priest must be a love-life and that priestly existence can help others to learn about love.[1]

---

1. William Luijpen's treatment of love in *Existential Phenomenology* (Pittsburgh: Duquesne University Press, 1969), pp. 311-26, is extraordinarily insightful. Parts of my treatment of love parallel his treatment.

I accept the view that love cannot really happen if people deal with one another totally in terms of their facticity. There are popular expressions that suggest that one person can love another person's facticity, but this love is not true. Though an individual might say, "I love your hair," or "I love your figure," this expression is not accurate. What the person means is, "I find your hair very attractive" or "I find your figure very beautiful," but in the richest sense of the word "love," one individual cannot love another's hair or figure. Quite simply, they are just not worth the gift of self that love requires. Love requires a commitment, and no one is going to make a commitment to someone else's hair or figure. There is no quality or determination or fact about one person that will call forth a gift of self from another. Only a self or a subjectivity will call forth that kind of gift.

For love to happen, one person must notice in however minimal a way the subjectivity of another. If I relate to all persons in terms of their facticity, their qualities, their determinations, then I will never love anyone. By locking other people into their facticity, I also lock myself into my facticity. I commit a kind of spiritual suicide: I become self-centered, which is just about the worst thing that a self can do. By using others, I not only hinder their development, I hinder my own development. I prevent the other from being present to me in a way that can deeply affect me and transform me. By reducing others to their roles or functions, I simultaneously identify myself with my role or function. Jewish philosopher Martin Buber has written incisively about this way of relating, which he refers to as I-It.

The man who has acquired an I and says I-It assumes a position before things but does not confront them in the current of reciprocity. He bends down to examine particulars under the objectifying magnifying glass of close scrutiny, or he uses the objectifying telescope of distant vision to arrange them as mere scenery . . . he experiences things as aggregates of qualities.[2]

To relate to another totally in terms of the other's facticity is to make love impossible.

CALLS AND NEEDS

If I notice the subjectivity of the other, I may become aware that the other is a need for me, a call to me, an appeal to me. We can discover this need by observing the nature of subjectivity. It is important to note that I am saying that the other *is* a need for me, *is* a call to me. I am talking about a need on the level of being rather than a need on the level of having. A need on the level of having can be satisfied by some thing. One person has five dollars and another person needs five dollars; one person has an automobile and another person needs an automobile. The ones who lack the five dollars and the automobile may call or appeal to the others for what they do not have. When I say a person *is* a need, a call, an appeal, I mean something more radical and existential than a need on the level of having. This need on the level of being cannot adequately be met by a response to a need on the level of having. Neither five dollars nor an automobile is a proper response to the call and need that every person is. The only proper response to that need is a gift of self.

---

2. Martin Buber, *I-Thou,* trans. Walter Kaufmann (New York: Scribner's, 1970), pp. 80-81.

If I respond on the level of having to a person as call and need, the person will have a sense of being cheated. An example can help to illustrate this point. Imagine that I finish a lecture at some parish. After my talk a person approaches, tells me how much she enjoyed my talk, and asks if she can see me some time in order to discuss a personal problem. I tell her to come to the college seminary the following Saturday afternoon. When the woman enters my room on Saturday she says, "Father, I really enjoyed your talk. You know I have this problem. . . ." I quickly interrupt her and tell her that I have just the book for her. I give her a book and whisk her out of the room. As she is leaving, she makes an appointment for the following week. On that occasion she says, "I enjoyed the book, but, you know, I still have a problem that I want to talk to you about." I do not allow her to finish speaking but hand her a new book and once again quickly dispatch her. Imagine that this type of meeting is repeated a few more times. The woman might make the following comment to one of her friends: "I've been seeing Father Lauder for several weeks, but I haven't really met him yet. He does have a wonderful library, and now I have most of it." The problem between the woman and me is that she is calling on the level of being and I am responding on the level of having. She rightly detects a kind of absence on my part. I may be physically present, but I am not present in the way that she needs. I am not present for her.

GIFT OF SELF

In this example suggesting the difference between calls and needs on the level of having and a call and need on the level of being, I have touched upon a central aspect of the mystery and meaning of love. I think love involves a special kind of presence. Using the insights of the French Catholic existentialist Gabriel Marcel, theologian John Macquarrie discusses the kind of presence that one person can bestow on another:

> The English word availability translates the French *disponibilité*: I must be willing to put myself at the disposal of the other. The sad truth, however, is that people are largely unavailable to one another. The unavailable person is preoccupied with himself and thus closed against the other. His existence is something that he "has," and his unavailability arises from his anxiety to maintain himself. But the way to genuinely human being lies through being open, through being able to expend oneself, and to do this generously or even extravagantly. There are clear echoes of New Testament teaching in these notions.
>
> It is in virtue of this kind of availability that one person is *present* to another. "Presence" writes Marcel "denotes something rather different and more comprehensive than the fact of just being there; to be quite exact, one should not actually say that an object is present." Presence depends on a person's coming out of himself or transcending himself toward the other.[3]

I doubt if there are any words that can adequately capture the activity of loving, but some words are better than others. Some possible expressions are: "I am at your service"; "I am present for you"; "My subjectivity is for your subjectivity"; "My personal presence is at the service of your freedom." The expression that is probably as good

---

3. John Macquarrie, *Existentialism* (London: Penguin, 1973), pp. 82-83.

as any is: "I am for you." That expression probably cap-
tures the mystery of loving as well as any. Love is the decision to be for someone else. Joseph Cardinal Ratzinger
said: "Being a Christian means essentially changing over
from being for oneself to being for one another."[4] Thus
love is at the heart of Christianity. Love is not the words,
"I love you" or "I am for you," but the gift of self to
another.

I suppose for most people most of the time their gift of
self is accompanied by very strong and pleasant feelings.
Obviously, this accompaniment occurs in romantic love. I
think it is rather important to distinguish the loving from
the feelings. A person can have all sorts of feelings and not
love; a person can love and have no feelings. I think one of
the more serious contemporary misunderstandings about
love is that people have identified love with feelings, emotions, and passions. People talk about "falling in love." I
find such expressions dangerous. If you can "fall in love,"
then you can "fall out of love." No one has complete control of his or her feelings. Emotions come and go, and
often we can understand neither their arrival nor their
departure.

I do not think love is either an emotion or a feeling. It is
a free choice. We love whom we choose to love, and we
love as long as we choose. Love is a self-gift that may be
accompanied by marvelously pleasing and fulfilling feelings. The key to love is that it is a self-gift that makes the
lover present to and for the loved one.

---

4. Quoted on the back cover of *Emmanuel* 86 (May 1980).

PRESENCE AS THE ESSENCE OF LOVE

Presence is the essence of love. If we discuss a dating pattern, this essence becomes obvious. The process goes something like this: a fellow and a girl go out one or two nights a month, then they go out every week, then two or three times a week. Finally, the young man is at his girl-friend's house almost every night. The girl's father may feel that he has taken in a new boarder. The reason this pattern takes place is that when we love people, we want to be present to them.

The experience of loving can reveal that this particular way of being present is especially fulfilling to the lover. In making oneself available to others, in giving self to others, the lover can discover the depths of his or her own personal existence. Lovers may see what most of us have to learn and relearn time and again: we are at our best when we are serving others; we are at our best when we are unselfish. We are often deceived into thinking that we will be fulfilled by gaining more and more possessions, by accumulating more and more things. We will never be fulfilled in this way. Only loving and being loved will fulfill us. The human heart will be fulfilled by nothing else. This is the way God has made us. Lovers can get a glimpse of this truth. They may discover the law of personal existence: by dying to ourselves, we live; by giving ourselves to others, we grow as selves; by helping others, our own personal existence is fulfilled. In loving others, we experience a kind of personal fullness and richness. We get a sense that whatever else personal existence means, its basic meaning is tied up with loving.

It is not just the activity of loving that fulfills us. The lovableness of the beloved fulfills us. The very presence and lovableness of the beloved are a kind of reward for us. Maurice Nédoncelle is especially astute on this point:

> There is a *minimum of reciprocity* in the fact that love originates in the perception of the lovableness of the beloved. If it is truly another that I love and not merely an impersonal quality pinned on him, it is he who, in a sense, has begun to love me. He has advanced me and enriched me simply by his very presence open to my perception. My love for him ought to begin in a kind of thanks, and I can tell him with the poet: *"C'est moi qui te dois tout, puisque c'est moi qui t'aime."* ("It is I who owe you everything, since it is I who love you.")
>
> It will be objected that this person does not even know that virtue has gone out of him, and he may be unaware of my existence. How can you say he is my benefactor? I answer: he has not willed me by name, he has not turned toward me as a result of a special decision, but he has given himself to the world, he has willed this in willing to display his activity and allow his personality to be glimpsed there.[5]

My own opinion is that every lover has some idea of what is good for the person or persons he or she loves. Every person who loves has some vision of what is good for the beloved. It may be a profound vision, or it may be a superficial vision. My idea of a profound vision would be to believe what is good for the beloved is that he or she share more deeply in the Risen Life of Christ, or that some day he or she encounter God and be united with him for all

---

5. Maurice Nédoncelle, *Love and the Person,* trans. Ruth Adelaide, S.C. (New York: Sheed and Ward, 1966), p. 19.

eternity. My idea of a superficial vision would be that the person amass an enormous amount of material wealth. Whatever the vision is that the lover has for the beloved, it involves the lover in a restraint that is difficult for most lovers. Because the very nature of the beloved is conscious freedom, the lover must want the beloved to freely fulfill the vision that the lover has for him or her or freely embrace what the lover thinks is good for the beloved. Why? To force some good on the beloved is to work against the very nature or essence of the beloved. The beloved is his or her freedom.

Nothing very valuable can happen to an adult that does not involve the adult's freedom. Either the adult must choose the good for himself or herself or at least affirm it after it occurs. I cannot make or force any adult to do anything that will be significant for the adult. For example, if I grab someone's arm, I can make the person cry, but there is no way that I can make the person be sorrowful or contrite. To be contrite involves a free choice. If I apply enough pressure to an individual's shoulders, I can force the person to kneel, but there is no way that I can force the person to worship. The only way that a person can worship is freely. If I have a sufficient amount of power and prestige, I can force people to act toward me in a certain way, perhaps even cause them to fawn over me, but there is no way that I can force people to love me. Love has to be free. There is no important activity that an adult engages in that is valuable for the person that does not involve the person's freedom. Belief, hope, love, contriteness, courage, prayer—name any personal activity that is of benefit to the one performing it—and it will be apparent that the person's freedom is involved.

PROPER DISTANCE

This freedom places a certain restraint on a lover. It also involves the lover in what is probably the most difficult aspect of human relationships: the proper distance. Most of us have great difficulty in achieving the proper distance from those we say we love. Either we are so distant that it is difficult to describe our relationship as love, or we are so close that it is difficult to respect the freedom of the other.

Two extreme examples may illustrate this point. Imagine that I am giving my last lecture to the graduating class of seniors at Cathedral College Seminary where I teach. As I am concluding my lecture I say, "I love all of you." Then I add, "But after you graduate, please don't come back to see me, don't write to me, don't call me on the phone. After you graduate, don't have any contact with me at all. As a matter of fact, if I never see you again it will be too soon!" The seniors would be quite justified in wondering about this strange type of loving. To them, it does not seem like loving at all, and they are quite right. I am placing such a distance between myself and them that it is silly to refer to our relationship as a love relationship. I am not going to be present to them in any way.

The second example can call attention to the other extreme: I am so present that I crush the freedom of the other. Imagine my saying goodbye to the same group of seniors. I say, "I love you"; then I add, "I want to give you copies of articles and books I have written. I'll be calling you regularly on the phone and dropping into your homes regularly for dinner. I'd like to give each of you ten or twelve photographs of myself to paste on the mirrors in your room. In fact, I have marvelous news for you: I love you so much that I'm going to form each of you into another me.'' Once again, there is a distance problem. I am refusing to respect the other's freedom. I wish to dominate and control.

The trick—and it does seem to require both skill and self-control—is to be genuinely interested and present to the other but to respect the other's freedom. The ideal is to be actively present but to keep hands off. This description of God may be one of the better ones we have. God is the one who is totally present but who keeps his hands off. God is totally and actively present to those he loves. God is more interested and concerned about us than we are about ourselves. God never departs. All talk about the absence of God is inaccurate; God is always present, but sometimes we are absent. God never forgets. However, God will not force us to obey him or return his love. God will not force us to worship, to hope, to be contrite, to believe, or to love. Because of the way that we are created by God, he would not force us to do any of these things. God has made a commitment to our freedom. He loves us so much, he loves our freedom so much, that he would never work against it. God loves us and respects us so much that, if we wish, he will allow us to reject him for all eternity. God respects our freedom more than we respect the freedom of one another. In a beautiful poem entitled *Freedom,* Charles Peguy pictures God speaking about his creatures' freedom:

> When you once have known what it is to be loved
> freely, submission no longer has any taste.
> All the prostrations in the world
> Are not worth the beautiful upright attitude of a free
> man as he kneels. All the submission, all the
> dejection in the world,

Are not equal in value to the soaring up point,
The beautiful straight soaring up of one single
   invocation
From a love that is free.[6]

LOVE IMITATES GOD

In loving people, we are trying to imitate God. Buber said: "Love is the godly in existence." In loving, we try to respect and affirm the freedom of others the way that God respects and affirms our freedom. In trying to define love, Nédoncelle zeroes in on the notion that love wills the good of the beloved.

> Among all the concepts attached to a given word we should choose the most authentic one, the one that can help us understand even the anomalies, twists and distortions to which the word is liable. Now, the concept that satisfies these requirements and that should enter into the definition we are looking for is the following: love is a will to promotion. The *I* that loves is willing above all the existence of the *thou*; it subsequently wills the autonomous development of the *thou*; and finally wills that this autonomous development be, if possible, in harmony with the value the *I* anticipates for the *thou*. Any other desire would be either a timid hesitation on the threshold of the temple or egoistic delight in a mirrored reflection. There is no love properly so-called unless there are two, and unless the *I* undertakes to go out to the *thou* in order to regard him in the truest possible sense, not as an object of curiosity, but as an interior existence having perfect subjectivity.[7]

6. Charles Peguy, "Freedom," in *God Speaks,* trans. Julian Green (New York: Pantheon, 1945), pp. 40-41.
7. Nédoncelle, p. 8.

In loving, we also imitate the creativity of God. In creating, God produces being from nothing. We do not do likewise, but in loving we do have a unique power to create those we love. We have the power to directly affect the subjectivity of the other so that the other becomes a new subjectivity. Of course, if the other does not accept our love, does not receive our self-gift, then the other is not created. But if the other accepts our gift of self, then the other has a possibility of growing and expanding in personal existence that the other could not have supplied for himself or herself. Why? The ultimate answer is that God has made us this way. He has made us so that we need one another. This need is the most radical meaning of coexistence. I cannot be me without you. On the most radical level of personal existence, I need the love of others, the self-gift of others, if I am going to grow as a self. My subjectivity needs the subjectivity of others. The gift of subjectivity, the gift of love offered to me, frees me so that I can transcend myself in a way I never could have done if the loving self of the other were not present.

An example may clarify the point I am trying to make about creativity. Imagine that I am invited to chaperon a teenage dance in a parish where one of my friends is a curate. I enter the gymnasium where the dance is taking place and begin to talk to my friend. As we are talking, I notice a young woman in a corner. I ask my friend, "Who is that?" My friend replies: "That is Lulu." I walk over and try to engage Lulu in a conversation. She is the most nervous, shy, self-conscious human being I have ever met. She is not at all physically attractive. Later my friend explains to me that Lulu attends the dances but just sits in a corner. Imagine that I am invited back to chaperon another dance in about six months. As soon as I enter the gymnasium, I look to the corner to see if Lulu is there. She is not. As I begin to talk to my friend, I notice a very attractive girl in the center of the dance floor. She is quite vivacious and seems to be the life of the party. I ask my friend who she is and he replies, "That's Lulu." I reply: "I can't believe it. That's Lulu? What happened to her?" My friend replies, "She met Louie!" Everyone else was reducing Lulu to her facticity. Everyone else was in various ways telling Lulu that she was "nothing but" her facticity. One human being, Louie, said, "I am for you," and he created her. Lovers are doing that to those they love all the time.

I do not think love is blind. I think love enables lovers to see what others of us may miss, namely that there is no such thing as an unlovable person. To be a person is to be lovable. Lovers see that. We have all been in situations similar to the following example. There is a family gathering. A nephew brings home his fiancée in order to introduce her to the clan. After they leave, all exchange glances and in effect say to one another, "What does he see in her?" They probably will never know what he sees in her. Love enables us to see what we cannot see without loving. When Jesus told us to love one another, he was calling us to enter reality more deeply. He was at least implicitly telling us the way things really are: people are lovable.

I also believe that love gives us some hint of the immortality of persons. Love enables us to at least suspect or hope for what the resurrection of Jesus reveals, namely that persons are made for eternity. In any experience of human death, everything in us tells us something is wrong. We have a sense that people should not die. Young people should not die; neither should old people. When we love others, we think that they should live forever. The resurrection of Jesus is like a love-explosion.[8] It reveals that love conquers even death. Marcel claimed that the experience of loving could reveal that the beloved will not die. Commenting on Marcel's philosophy and quoting from him, Kenneth Gallagher writes:

> In so far as love, even of a creature, bears on a thou, it rises beyond the entire order of things and of the destruction which preys upon things: "Love only addresses itself to what is eternal, it immobilizes the beloved above the world of genres and vicissitude." To love a being, as we have seen, is to say to him: "Thou at least shalt not die." It will do no good to say that nevertheless he will die, since all things come to an end, for the prophetic affirmation of love is precisely a proclamation that the beloved as beloved is exempt from the penalties of thingness: the fate which lies in wait for things cannot overtake "that by which being is truly a being." The more we love him, the more we comprehend him as authentic being, the more we can be assured of his perpetuity. At the limit where total assurance becomes possible, it could only be because his thingness is swallowed up in an absolute and indefectible presence. Really to love a creature, Marcel would agree, is to love him in God. Only in the absolute does the promise of eternity with which all love is redolent attain to unconditionality. This is not a matter of inference or argumentation: it simply means that our experience of presence is truncated and our assurance sapped unless they arise within an enveloping absolute.

8. I discuss the resurrection as a love explosion in more detail in *The Love Explosion: Human Experience and the Christian Mystery* (Locust Valley, N.Y.: Living Flame Press, 1979).

Not only perfect love but all love insofar as it *is* love, is haunted by this illimitable presence. That is the meaning of the prophetic "thou shalt not die": through my love I grasp you as participant in a presence which cannot fail. The more I love you, the surer I am of your eternity: the more I grow in authentic love for you, the deeper becomes my trust and faith in the Being which founds your being.[9]

Jesus' resurrection confirms the experience of lovers that suggests the beloved will not die.

LEVELS OF LOVING

I know from experience that most people are interested in love. However, when something of the beauty and excitement of love is unveiled, very soon the question is raised: "But how many people can you love? How many close relationships can you sustain?" The question is an excellent one. It calls our attention to the truth that there are all sorts of levels in loving, all sorts of degrees of intensity. Some people are capable of sustaining a number of intimate personal relationships; some people have difficulty sustaining one. I think a lot of factors influence how many people one individual can have close relationships with: the individual's physical and emotional stamina, the amount of free time available to the individual, and, most importantly in my view, the level of freedom that the individual has achieved. I knew a priest who seemed to be capable of sustaining a large number of relationships. He was the freest man I have ever met. He could counsel people all day long. He was always giving of him-

---

9. Kenneth Gallagher, *The Philosophy of Gabriel Marcel* (New York: Fordham University Press, 1962), p. 80.

self. He seemed to have worked out his own problems and was now free to be for others. However, as free as he was, I once heard that he said, "I have the feeling that people are eating me." There is no doubt that love relationships can be tremendously demanding.

To how many people can I give myself in love? To how many people can I be available? While it is true that an individual can have close love relationships with only a few people, I believe that, because there are different levels of loving, it is possible to love everyone. Nothing that we have said about love needs to be sacrificed in order to accept that I can love everyone. When I suggest that we should try to love everyone, I mean that we should have at least a minimal attitude of being for a person, of being in favor of that person. If the opportunity arose, we would do what we could and be present for that person. Just as in an intense love relationship, the lover is changed and becomes aware of a new level of his or her own personal existence, so in trying to assume even a minimal loving stance toward everyone, the lover touches a new level of his or her own personal existence. He or she will become a saint.

A PRIEST'S LOVE

Every aspect of the phenomenology of love presented here can be applied to priestly existence. Placed within the context of Christian revelation, every aspect of the phenomenology of love takes on a new depth and a new importance. By trying to live a life of Christian love, the priest calls others to live that type of existence.

The priest believes that every person he meets is a call to him, an appeal to him, a need for him. The call can be translated: "Be with me, help me to grow, help me to be more free." But in the light of Christian revelation, it can mean something even more profound: "Help me to be like Jesus, help me to share in Jesus' risen life, help me to be a Christian." The priest believes that this call, whether the people he encounters know it or not, is what their very being means. To be a subjectivity in God's plan of redemption is to be a call, a need, an appeal for union with the Risen Christ. This is true of all people, even those who consciously profess that they do not believe in Jesus.

If the priest responds in love, he is giving himself in service to those he loves; he is making himself available in love to those he serves. But because of the Risen Christ's presence to him in grace, and also through the sacrament of orders that he has received, the priest can bring an especially rich presence to people. St. Paul, discussing his own existence, said: "I live now not I, but Christ lives in me." As he gives himself in loving service, the priest cannot help but give the Risen Lord also.

The priest has a vision of what is good for those he loves. He wants them to become more and more like Jesus and more and more open to the Father's self-gift. He also wants them to be part of God's kingdom for all eternity. However, the priest should see that this goal can happen only through the free cooperation of those he loves. The priest then exists in a special kind of tension. Trying to imitate Jesus, the priest is present to those he loves, but he cannot force them to follow the vision he has for them. I know when I was newly ordained and working as a parish priest, I found this tension very difficult. As I look back, I see that I would be present to people as long as they did what I wanted them to do but that I withdrew my presence when they did not respond. I also realize that I was manipulative with people in trying to get them to do what I thought was good for them. I was so present to them that I tried to *make* them do what I wanted. The other extreme is to be so distant from them that you have no interest in them at all. It is difficult to be so present that you are actively involved but still "keep your hands off."

Certainly, the love that animates priestly existence should help a priest to see what others may miss seeing. The priest believes that all persons are so precious that God's Son died for them. Not only is the priest's love not blind, but it is illumined by Christian faith. It sees the infinite value of persons. It also sees that love through Jesus' resurrection has conquered death.

The priest's love is creative. It may at least occasionally be creative not just of persons but of Christian persons. When the priest's vision is freely embraced, freely affirmed by those he loves, the new fullness that they achieve, the new depth that they experience, may be specifically related to Christian personhood. In other words, the priest's loving presence may help a person to accept consciously the Father's loving gift of self.

More than any other vocation I can think of, priesthood deals with the subjectivity of people. Like anyone else, a priest can slip into dealing with people on the level of facticity. Yet this level really contradicts the meaning of his vocation. The priest is supposed to be a man for others, that is to say, a priest is one who loves.

Married life is one way of loving, and celibacy is another way of loving. In *The Sexual Celibate*, Donald Goergen defines Christian celibacy as "a positive choice of the single life for the sake of Christ in response to the call of God."[10] Goergen goes on to say:

> There are many reasons why one might choose to be single, e.g., in order to be a playboy. To choose celibate singleness, however, is to put one's life and one's freedom in the context of a particular response to God. There are two major dimensions to celibate life: a positive choice of all that is implied in the single life as well as putting this choice in the context of the Christian vocation. One does not choose the single life for itself alone; he or she chooses it for the sake of Christ.[11]

Whatever the merits of married clergy, celibacy should help the priest to love and should free him to be lovingly present to the community.

---

10. Donald Goergen, *The Sexual Celibate* (New York: Seabury, 1974), pp. 108-109.
11. Ibid., p. 109.

VII

THE PRIEST:
A DYNAMIC, LOVING PRESENCE

One of the positive things about my job of teaching contemporary philosophy to college seminarians is that I am
trying to teach students thought currents that have already
influenced their thinking. Though the material may never
have been presented to them formally in a classroom, both
they and I discover that they have some familiarity with at
least some of it. My sympathy goes out to professors who
must present ancient or medieval philosophy to contemporary students. The task before them is especially difficult because of the students' lack of familiarity with the
ancient and medieval worlds. Contemporary philosophy
has deeply influenced the world in which the students live.
I find that the philosophy of priesthood that I have
presented in this book is more than compatible with a
number of contemporary, specifically Catholic, articulations concerning priestly existence. Perhaps this compati-
bility should not be surprising since this philosophy is

drawn from contemporary philosophy, especially existentialism. The philosophy of priesthood that I have outlined in this book echoes much of what is being said about priestly existence by theologians and in Church documents. In this final chapter, a discussion of the five aspects of personal existence previously addressed (person and world, person and truth, person and freedom, person and community, and person and love) will now be directed only toward priestly existence. This discussion will serve several purposes. It will review, reemphasize, and expand what has been said already. It will also underline the practical aspect of this philosophy. Philosopher Robert Johann writes:

> Ideas have consequences; they are plans for action. Any mistake in the plans is inevitably an obstacle to growth. What a man believes—about himself, about the world, about God—will control the way he develops, the richness (or poverty) of his life.[1]

In dealing with these five aspects of priestly existence, we will try to keep in mind that everything that the priest does has a double dimension: it enriches his own existence but also at least indirectly the existence of those to whom he ministers. The nature of priestly existence is to be for others. We wish to avoid suggesting any spiritual schizophrenia for the priest by separating his personal existence from his ministry or separating his personal holiness from his apostolate. The Vatican II "Decree on the Ministry and Life of Priests" stresses that the priest's mission is his meaning, that through service to others the priest will grow as a person. The decree declares:

---

1. Robert Johann, *Building the Human* (New York: Herder and Herder, 1968), p. 55.

Priests will acquire holiness in their own distinctive way by exercising their functions sincerely and tirelessly in the Spirit of Christ. Since they are the ministers of the Word of God, they read and hear every day the Word of God that they must teach to others. If they strive at the same time to make it part of their own lives, they will become daily more perfect disciples of the Lord, according to the saying of the Apostle Paul to Timothy: "Meditate on these things, give thyself entirely to them, that thy progress may be manifest to all. Take heed to thyself and to thy teaching; be earnest in them. For in so doing thou will save both thyself and those that hear thee" (1 Tim. 4: 15-16). For by seeking more effective ways of conveying to others what they have meditated, they will savor more profoundly the "unfathomable riches of Christ" (Eph. 3:8) and the many-sided wisdom of God.[2]

By living priestly existence in all its depth and richness, a priest will grow as a person as he helps others. Perhaps it would be more accurate to say he will grow as a person through helping others.

UNVEILING ULTIMATE MEANING

Part of a priest's mission is to call people into a new world of meanings in order to open up new horizons for them. This truth was always important. Today it may be more important than ever. The world that the priest tries to unveil for others is a world of ultimate meaning. Contemporary persons have many such worlds offered to them.

---

2. "Decree on the Ministry and Life of Priests of Vatican Council II," in *Vatican Documents* (Glen Rock, N.J.: Paulist Press, 1966), pp. 133-34.

One of the most popular is the world of meaning that we have described as secular. In *Unsecular Man*, Andrew Greeley argues that contemporary man is looking for ultimate meaning and is freer in making his religious choices: "All that we are asserting is that, relatively speaking, the individual in contemporary society not only enjoys more religious options but is much freer of communal constraint in exercising his options than were his ancestors."[3]

Thus the priest's task is especially exciting and challenging. Believing that the Christian world of meaning contains the deepest meanings, the priest must help his contemporaries share this belief. This task is important and difficult. Greeley stresses our freedom in choosing a world of meanings or a horizon.

> On the other hand, if he is free of communal constraint he is also free of communal support. Freedom is a two edged sword; while it enhances the personal control of the individual, it also increases his responsibility. If there has been an increase in the range of relatively free decisions in human life, it has to be considered a blessing. But it is not an unmixed blessing, or at least not a painless one. When options are made available to us, we must choose; when the constraints of the community which would direct us toward a choice are lessened, then we must choose by ourselves.[4]

The contemporary priest must so unveil the world of faith that he will help contemporary persons freely to choose that world. The priest need not be concerned about

---

3. Andrew Greeley, *Unsecular Man: The Persistence of Religion* (New York: Schocken Books, 1972), p. 73.
4. Ibid.

the intrinsic attractiveness of the world of faith. That world, that horizon of meaning, is the most attractive in the history of the human race. The priest's task is to help his contemporaries see it in all its beauty and attractiveness so that they will be encouraged to embrace it freely.

In proclaiming God's Word—whether it be in the pulpit, in the confessional, in the classroom, in the rectory office, or wherever—the priest is trying to open the world of faith-meanings to people, trying to extend the horizons of people to include the meanings of Christian revelation. He is either calling people into the world of faith or calling them to be present more deeply and dynamically to it. This effort on the part of the priest is one of the key sources of his own holiness. If he is authentically calling people, then he must be authentically present to that world. Indeed, his own faith horizon will strongly influence how well or how poorly he unveils faith-meanings for others. The priest's spiritual life is intimately tied to the way he serves people. The priest's ministry to people is a ministry of the word. The greatness of a ministry of the word and the intimate relation between a priest's sanctity and service to the word is expressed in *As One Who Serves*:

> Proclaiming the word of God is preaching, instruction in Catholic faith, teaching, speaking in faith to contemporary problems, witnessing as a person of faith in the world.
>
> The word of God is sacred scripture, and yet more, because even the scriptures are testimony that God has spoken. What God has said to all people is Jesus Christ, the Word-made-flesh (Heb. 1:1-3). He came to proclaim God's word. He is God's word. That word becomes fully available in the Church and the one whom the Church sends (Rom. 10:15). The min-

istry of the word of God is truly a primary expression of priestly and diaconal ministry.

God, then, continues to speak Christ to the world in the spirit. The Spirit is present when the priest or deacon proclaims for the benefit of the community that Christ is the goal and meaning of life, the only measure of behavior, the only light in which to make choices. In this prophetic ministry, the priest or deacon will still discern only imperfectly because he, too, continues to grow in faith, hope and prayer. But even this struggle to hear the word and keep it is itself a form of proclamation.[5]

PROCLAIMING CHRISTIAN TRUTH

The absolutely indispensable role that a priest has in society as a minister of the word is made more clear when what has been said about truth is related to a priest's ministry. Having made a commitment to the truth of the Christ-event, the priest calls others to make a commitment. All truth changes the knower, but no truth can transform so profoundly or radically as the truth of Christian revelation.

In *Sign of Contradiction,* the book based on a series of spiritual exercises he gave before he became Pope John Paul II, Karol Wojtyla writes about truth:

> Thus it is truth that makes man what he is. His relationship with truth is the deciding factor in his human nature and it constitutes his dignity as a person. At the same time that relationship with truth— an inner relationship, certainly, but one which also

5. *As One Who Serves: Reflections on the Pastoral Ministry of Priests in the United States* (Washington, D.C.: United States Catholic Conference, 1977), p. 42.

expresses itself externally—is an integral part of the
"mystery of man"; this finds confirmation in Christ
the prophet (Lk. 7:16).[6]

There is no doubt that this inner relationship that makes
man what he is expresses itself externally. Truth changes a
person's life. Christian truth can dramatically change a
person's life. Wojtyla stresses the role of Christ the prophet and the essential role of truth in human existence:

> Christ, the great prophet, is the one who proclaims
> divine truth and he is also the one who shows the dig-
> nity of man to be bound up with truth: with truth
> honestly sought, earnestly pondered, joyfully ac-
> cepted as the greatest treasure of the human spirit,
> witnessed to by word and deed in the sight of man.
> Truth has a divine dimension; it belongs by nature
> to God himself; it is one with the divine Word. At the
> same time it constitutes an essential dimension of
> human knowledge and human existence, of science,
> wisdom and the human conscience. Every man is
> born into the world to bear witness to the truth ac-
> cording to his own particular vocation.[7]

The priest's vocation is to bear witness to the deepest,
most meaningful, and most enriching truth. To people
searching for some meaning to human existence and some
goal for the human heart's yearning, the priest proclaims
that God is a Father. To accept that truth is to be liberated.
In the *cursillo* movement there is an expression used to suggest the freedom of the Christian: "My father is a millionaire." The implication is that the child of a millionaire
has no worries. That God is our Father means that we have

---

6. Karol Wojtyla, *Sign of Contradiction* (New York: Seabury,
1979), p. 119.
7. Ibid., p. 120.

a God who is more interested in us than we are in ourselves. This truth, if accepted, has an enormous power to change someone's life.

To people searching for some meaning in spite of the inevitability of death, the priest proclaims the Risen Jesus. Not only is death not the end of personal existence, but because of Jesus' loving sacrificial self-gift, death has become the entrance to human fulfillment. It is difficult to imagine a more radical truth. To accept it is to look on all human experience differently.

To contemporary people who feel down and even abandoned in a seemingly meaningless universe, the priest proclaims the presence of Jesus' Spirit. Not only are we not abandoned, but we have the Spirit of Love animating us, modeling us to be like the Risen Lord.

There is so much truth to Christian revelation that the priest will never exhaust its meaning and mystery either for himself or others. His experience of proclaiming Christian truth should lead to a deepening of his own grasp of it and commitment to it. Of course, even as the priest is trying to unveil truth to another, he may find that the other is simultaneously unveiling truth to him. This mutual unveiling has happened frequently to me with a close friend of mine. She is a student in social work and intensely interested in social problems. However, until she and I began to speak about social issues, she had no idea that the Catholic Church had a detailed social doctrine. Though she had more than twelve years of Catholic education, the Church's social teaching had never been unveiled for her. Now I find that as I explain the Church's social teaching to her, she is able to explain the concrete complexity of a social problem to me in a way that I would not see without her help. Through our mutual interaction, we are helping one another see more deeply into the truth of social justice.

The whole area of social justice may be one whose truth is not known by large numbers of Catholics who know other aspects of the Church's teaching extremely well. As an apostle of truth, the contemporary priest may have a special mission concerning that area. The document *As One Who Serves* stresses the priest's commitment to the social truth taught by the Church:

> The priest is above all aware of his duty of educating the people of the parish to a sense of both national and international justice. For the specific contribution of Christians to justice is the day-to-day life of the individual believer acting like the Gospel leaven in his family, his school, his work, his social and civic life. Included with this are the perspectives of meaning which the faithful can give to human effort. Accordingly, educational method must be such as to teach people to live life in its entire reality and in accord with the evangelical principles of personal and social morality which are expressed in a vital Christian witness. But this education demands a renewal of heart, a renewal based on the recognition of sin in its individual and social manifestations.
>
> The priest can be expected to assure that this dimension is incorporated in all programs of education in the parish. He supports the efforts of the social justice committee of the parish council, advising them of statements at national and universal levels concerning questions of war, nuclear arms, support for the United Nations, strip-mining, world hunger, and a vast array of issues. His role includes cooperating with and coordinating services offered at the diocesan level to meet the call for justice.[8]

8. *As One Who Serves*, pp. 52-53.

In trying to unveil the truth of the Church's social teaching to people or, indeed, in trying to unveil any of the truths of Christian revelation to people, the priest is necessarily calling people to a deeper freedom. All truth frees us. All truth opens doors for us and leads us fruitfully into the future. Because no other truth or set of truths is so profound as the truths of Christian revelation, people have a special opportunity to become more free by committing themselves to Christian truth.

CALLING PEOPLE TO A
FREEDOM IN COMMUNITY

In his ministry, whether he is dealing with children of grammar school age or people celebrating thirty or more years of marriage, the priest is calling people to a deeper freedom. The popular view that commitment destroys freedom could not be further from the truth. Sartre and other contemporary atheists have insisted that if there were a God, human persons would not be free. The opposite is closer to the truth: through a life-commitment in faith to God, a person can approach the deepest level of freedom. By finding God, we find ourselves. By choosing God, we exercise our freedom in the most profound manner. Everything about a priest's existence should say these truths to people. I suppose the pivotal example to which we can point is the resurrection of Jesus. The Gospel scene in the Garden of Gethsemane suggests that in the near future Jesus' freedom will be forfeited. He will be taken prisoner and die. What could be less freeing? Yet Jesus in faith commits himself to his Father. Death, which seems to be the destruction of freedom, becomes the fulfillment of freedom. Jesus' humanity is so fulfilled and freed in his risen life that he can now be present in love in all places at all times to all people. A life commitment in faith to God is not only a profound exercise of freedom, but such a commitment can lead to the deepest kind of free personal existence.

The priest's own free commitment and fidelity to the Lord releases him to freely serve others. This commitment does not bind the priest in chains but rather fulfills his humanity. We grow as persons by giving ourselves away; we live by dying to ourselves; we develop as selves by being interested in other selves. Besides the sign of his own free commitment, the priest preaches the liberating Word of God. Our choices make us who we are. By preaching and proclaiming God's Word to people, the priest is inviting them to become whom God has called them to be. In every choice, we create ourselves to some extent. In choosing God's Word, in opening ourselves to Christ's truth, we make ourselves, we achieve to some extent the freedom of the children of God. We have many false images of ourselves. All of them, because they are fallacious, are to some extent unfreeing. Some, to the extent that we really accept them, are seriously unfreeing. I believe that the secular image of personal existence is unfreeing.[9] The image of ourselves that Christian revelation offers is most freeing. What could free us more than believing that we are so lovable that God sent his Son to die for us? What could free us more than believing God sent his Spirit to be lovingly and constantly present to us? What could free us more than believing the image of a loving Father that Jesus pro-

---

9. I do not mean that secularists are unfree in their actions. I mean that the secular vision in comparison to the Christian vision is stunted and hence to that extent unfreeing.

vides for us in the Gospels? What could free us more than believing that we are intimately united with Father, Son, and Spirit through grace? What could free us more than believing that God wants an eternity of happiness for us? What truth of Christian revelation does not have the power to free us? The priest spends his life calling people to accept God's truth. He spends his life trying to help people allow their conscience and consciousness to be Christlike, that is to say, a priest spends his life calling people to freedom.

The freedom to which the priest calls people is a freedom in community, a community of disciples.

> Discipleship, as a way of life, then, is the basic spirituality of the servant People of God. That spirituality will vary in form and emphasis because the Church is a living reality and its response in each age bears the stamp of its own life in that generation. However it develops, the spirituality remains the work of one and the same Spirit (I Cor. 12:11). With hope in the Lord rather than itself, the Servant Church lives and works at the frontiers of time and change, confident that the Lord of history will bring to completion the good work He started in it (Phil. 1:6).[10]

One of the key signs that the Christian community offers to the world is that it is a community of love. Everyone co-exists; Christians try to coexist in love. They attempt to avoid the temptation of reducing one another to facticity, of reducing one another to a function or a role. The members of the community try in various ways to free one another. Though not easy, this goal is magnificent: a com-

---

10. *As One Who Serves*, p. 13.

munity of free people who through care and concern try to further liberate one another. The priest attempts to keep this model before himself and before others. Henri Nouwen is strongly critical of Christian ministers who embrace a kind of individualism:

> One of the most conspicuous forms of faithlessness in the ministry is the blatant individualism of the ministers. Seminaries often seem to be grounds for individual stardom. But Jesus did not send His disciples out one by one. He ordered them to go out together. . . . Much competition and rivalry within the ministry, as well as much of the loneliness and frustration of ministers, find their basis in rugged individualism.[11]

Today an increasing number of priests seem to see the importance of community not only for their flock but for themselves. They seem to sense that individualism in all its forms leads to decline rather than growth. An encouraging sign is the number of priest fraternities, prayer groups, and discussion groups in existence in this country. Another encouraging sign is that young priests especially seem to have a strong sense of the importance of sharing ministry with lay people. How to do so in a given situation can be difficult, but awareness of its importance is a step in the right direction.

A MINISTRY OF LOVE

As a leader in a community of love, the priest is called to a ministry of love. The secret of human fulfillment lies in the mystery of loving and being loved. At least as much as

---

11. Henri Nouwen, "The Monk and the Cripple," *America* 142 (March 15, 1980): 206.

any other state in life, the meaning of the priesthood is tied up with that mystery. Wojtyla states:

> The human will—or rather the human heart—impels man to be "for others," to have generous relationships with others. It is in this that the essential structure of personal and human existence consists. Man exists not merely "in the world," not merely "in himself," he exists "in relationship," "in self-giving." Only through disinterested giving of himself can man attain to full discovery of himself. More than anything else the priesthood, linked with celibacy by Gospel precepts and centuries-old tradition, gives expression to this truth about man. The priesthood in particular is the form of self-expression of the man for whom the world's ultimate meaning can be found only in the dimension of the transcendental: in turning towards God who, as fullness of personal Being, in himself transcends the world.[12]

At the end of the chapter on love, I tried to connect priestly existence to all the aspects of love that had been discussed. This connection seems especially important in emphasizing that the priest's vocation is a ministry of love to relate priestly existence to the Eucharist and to risen life beyond death. In a special way, the Eucharist sums up the meaning of priestly ministry and makes clear that it is a ministry of love. Everything important about the priest's person and mission is suggested in a Eucharistic celebration. The priest calls the congregation to receive God's Word, which is the truth that liberates them. He calls them together as a community of people who freely express their faith and freely commit themselves to the Lord. The priest celebrates a banquet of love with the community, a ban-

---

12. Wojtyla, p. 132.

quet that calls the community to loving service. The following quotation echoes what I have been saying:

> It is in the Eucharist that the priest finds the full experience and expression of his person and ministry. He receives nourishment, hope, and life itself from the Table of God's Holy Word and the Table of God's Sacred Bread. He stands under His Word, learning its challenge to discipleship. In proclaiming that Word, he integrates his person and its power. His very person emits a servant leadership as he calls the people to worship, and as he calls forth leaders through the variety of ministries coordinated in service. He senses his oneness with the people in the expression of repentance, the prayer of the faithful, and the sign of Peace. It is in this consciousness of self and others in unity that he comes to know and appreciate the need for and effects of his ministry for justice.[13]

The Eucharist, the sign of God's love, is also the sign of the priest's ministry of love. What takes place in sacrament and sign in a Eucharistic liturgy, the priest tries to live out in his daily existence.

Reflection on the nature of the love that the priest tries to embody and on the community that the priest serves can reveal similarity between the Divine Community of the Trinity and the community of Jesus' followers. *Gaudium et Spes* states:

> Indeed, the Lord Jesus, when He prayed to the Father, "that all may be one . . . as we are one" (Jn. 17:21-22) opened up vistas closed to human reason. For He implied a certain likeness between the union of the divine Persons, and in the union of God's sons in truth and charity. This likeness reveals that man,

---

13. *As One Who Serves,* pp. 72-73.

who is the only creature on earth which God willed for itself, cannot fully find himself except through a sincere gift of himself.[14]

Referring to this text Wojtyla comments:

The vocation to communion—in which persons offer one another gifts of truth and love as in the case of the divine Persons—is deeply ingrained in man. The Son of God came into this world in order to reveal to mankind this sublime vocation to unity in truth by way of charity. That is why Jesus declared charity to be the greatest of all the commandments, making it central to his Gospel (Mk. 12:28-31) and predicting that it would determine his final judgment (Mt. 25:34-35).[15]

The priest's ministry mirrors that of Jesus: revealing "to mankind this sublime vocation to truth by way of charity." The love that animates the Christian community is a love that will conquer even death. Beyond death, the Christian community will reach its fulfillment with the Community of Persons it tries to model. The priest's loving service is a sign not only of love on earth but love beyond the grave.

Concluding his reflections on personal existence in *Who Is Man?*, Abraham Heschel writes:

Who is man? A *being in travail with God's dreams and designs*, with God's dream of a world redeemed, of reconciliation of heaven and earth, of a mankind which is truly His image, reflecting His wisdom, justice and compassion. God's dream is not to be alone, to have mankind as a partner in the drama of continuous creation. By whatever we do, by every act we

---

14. *Gaudium et Spes,* n. 24.
15. Wojtyla, p. 178.

carry out, we either advance or obstruct the drama of redemption; we either reduce or enhance the power of evil.[16]

I believe Heschel's insights into personal existence have special application to a priest. He is a being in travail with God's dreams and designs. The priest has been made a partner of the Lord and is at the heart of the drama of redemption.

Philosophy is a reflection on human experience. At its most profound, philosophy deals with mystery. Philosophizing about priestly existence reveals the most exciting and inspiring truths. Such philosophizing helps us to see more deeply into the mystery of priesthood. It also reveals what most priests know from experience, namely, that among life's options priestly existence is a marvelous way to spend a life.

---

16. Abraham Heschel, *Who Is Man?* (Palo Alto, Calif.: Stanford University Press, 1965), p. 119.

PRAYER

Father, we are called by you through Jesus Christ, your Son. Through his priesthood we become your missioners, your messengers, your meaning-givers. Today we stand tall, Father, and in faith we recall the meaning of our priestly ministry.

Father, your Son's presence reaches out to people, your Son's concern consoles people, your Son's life transforms people, your Son's love liberates people. Through special devotions, national customs, and ritual blessings, your grace sanctifies people. The Incarnation begun two thousand years ago in Judea continues in the United States, in Canada and Europe, in India and Korea, in Africa and Latin America. In season and out of season, Christ reaches out through his ministers, through us, to touch people: on every corner and on every avenue; in schools and in administration; in gymnasiums and old age homes; in churches, convents, and seminaries; at each moment and in every place; to every race and nationality—the incarnate loving Lord reaches to minister to people.

Father, in the mystery of your providence, you have decided to involve us, to use us, to send us. Like Isaiah, each of us, perhaps in fear and trembling, but also in trust and confidence, has answered your call by saying, "Here I am, send me." Today we answer again, "Adsum, I am ready."

141

The stains of sin and the strains of the human struggle around us almost suffocate us. The needs are enormous. No service is sufficient. Pain requires presence.

Priesthood means presence:
the presence of Jesus through our presence;
the words of Jesus through our lips;
the healing of Jesus through our hands;
the heart of Jesus through our hope;
the compassion of Jesus through our consoling;
the joy of Jesus through our joy;
the love of Jesus through our sharing;
the "yes" of Jesus through our "yes."

Father, the "yes" of service has many forms: profound and simple; planning and doing; athletic, pragmatic, artistic. Priesthood means saying "yes." It means saying "yes" to you, Father, and ministering to others so that "yes" echoes throughout the world. We say "yes" to you, Father, and by our lives we try to help others to say "yes"

"yes" in the early years when conscience is formed and values are planted;
"yes" in the late years when age hints that death may be near and loneliness almost crushes;
"yes" in the moments of joy when God seems near;
"yes" in the moments of sadness when God seems absent;
"yes" in a ministry when even one's life must be surrendered;
"yes" in a hospital when discouragement is threatening;
"yes" in the prisons when hope seems distant;
"yes" through the commitment of marriage;

"yes" through the courage of Confirmation;
"yes" through penance in the rite of reconciliation;
"yes" in the breaking of the bread.

With our lives we minister to others helping them to say "yes." With our lives, and in a special way today, we place ourselves as priests in your presence, and we say "yes."

Other books by the author:

Hope: A Christian Response to Chicken Little

*The Love Explosion: Human Experience
and the Christian Mystery*

Loneliness Is for Loving

*Income derived from the sale of Affirmation books is applied to
providing care for clergy and religious suffering from emotional
unrest.*

AFFIRMATION BOOKS is an important part of the ministry of
the House of Affirmation, International Therapeutic Center for
Clergy and Religious, founded by Sr. Anna Polcino, S.C.M.M.,
M.D.